COACHING
FROM A
PROFESSED
Hot Mess

Tips on
Life, Love, Dating,
Online Dating
Female Empowerment
& LGBT Support
from a
Board Certified
Life Coach,
TV Dating Expert
& Hot Mess

BROOKE LEWIS

outskirtspress
DENVER, COLORADO

Outskirts Press, Inc.
http://www.outskirtspress.com

ISBN: 978-1-4787-7710-6

Outskirts Press and the "OP" logo are trademarks belonging to Outskirts Press, Inc.

CONTENTS

HOT MESS

Urban Dictionary Definition:

Defined, "hot mess" refers to when a "person's appearance is in a state of total disarray while still maintaining an undeniable attractiveness" & allure.

Hot messes' are appealing for a variety of reasons, most notably because they're generally unexpected, capricious, & agonizingly provocative. Additionally, numerous contingent factors make duplication rare and continual repetition virtually impossible.

No one set of guidelines can perpetually determine what distinguishes a "hot mess" from an above-average train wreck. Regardless of the circumstances, you know it when you see it; because they are typically conspicuous, and obviously they are always awesome.

INTRODUCTION

LIFE CAN BE crazy! So, in 2016, I chose to embrace my "crazy" and use my blessed and beautiful bedside table book to profess..."I am a HOT MESS!" Yup...I said it, rock it and OWN IT! Now, being an Actress, Life Coach and Dating Expert in the public eye, some may think I am really "crazy" sharing this with the world! I know some of you are thinking (and, judging!) that a Board Certified Life and Dating Coach, professional and working actress should not "air her dirty laundry." Well, I cannot tell you how good it feels to be self-aware enough to admit and embrace my "flaws". Along with my strengths, my "flaws" and weaknesses make me vulnerable, special and unique. I also believe that by sharing my HOT MESS quirks with you, it will support you in embracing your HOT MESS quirks, too! Let's break the 'rules' and stop chasing "perfection". It gets tiring trying to be "perfect" all the time, doesn't it?

Speaking of tired, I am *exhausted!* Now, I am not even referring to the type of exhausted that comes from my having chronic health issues, since childhood or chronic *Epstein-Barr Virus* and *Fibromyalgia*, since college. I am talking about the kind of mental, emotional and physical exhaustion that comes from being a single woman (or, woman in general!), having multiple careers, working in the public eye, living in Hollywood, being an actress and trying to please all the family, friends and fans I am blessed with! I realize I have several jobs, but sometimes I feel like I have several hundred (I know you are totally relating right now!). I am tired of working so hard! I am tired of trying to be "perfect" and please everyone! I'm tired of caring so much about what people think of me! I'm tired of trying to be something I'm not! Worst of all, I am tired of trying to please MYSELF (Yes, readers, I am cursed as a perfectionistic, self-critical *Virgo*!). My family, friends and reps will tell you I am my own worst enemy! I have forced myself, at times, to live up to some crazy "standard" that I have placed upon myself. Even as a Board Certified Life Coach, with a lifetime of therapists, coaches and healers of my own, I still buy into the propaganda, media, internet, social media insanity and B.S. of Hollywood. I am tired of comparing myself to actresses who are naturally skinny. I'm tired of being on a diet. I'm tired of engaging in ridiculous conversations around how many followers I have on *Twitter* and *Instagram*! I mean, when did our value as people and professionals become based on social media? And, any professional actors, producers, directors or writers reading this, when did we stop getting hired for jobs, because our ranking on *IMDB* went above 10,000? I think all this pressure would make any sane person stressed and "crazy"! And, don't even get me started with online dating (LOL)! Online dating can test your sanity beyond measure! I'm so tired of trying to please random strangers who want to "see more body shots", text for hours on end and send the always offensive "d*ck" pics! And, I am beyond spent from meeting men for a drink who look nothing like their photos and want to add 10 years to their listed ages (I know all you online daters are either laughing or crying right now!). The light at the end of my tunnel is that I have found the courage and inner strength to make powerful choices and push through these challenges and exhaustion. I'm still here and I am still standing! I only hope my opening up and sharing my HOT MESS will encourage you to find energy and strength to push through your challenges too!

Now, as a Board Certified Life Coach and someone who has studied metaphysics and spirituality for many years, I am committed to living my life as integrous and authentically, as possible (while, still OWNING my HOT MESS!). We want to commit to being our best, doing our best and making the most powerful choices we can make in each moment and experience we are given. Does that mean being "perfect"? No way! It just means being powerful! One of my favorite coaching theories (you will hear me speak and write about this often!) that I learned in a "power of the mind" course many years ago is, "There is a lot of power in our choices!" With every choice, there is a consequence (meaning a result!), so we really do have some power in the results we see in our lives. As a Life Coach and someone who has a stable of gifted coaches supporting me, I have acquired the tools to support others in dealing with the issues they are facing and making powerful choices. Will we all fall, fail or make mistakes again at some point? Of course! In fact, we will make mistakes and do crazy things for the rest of our lives…that's LIFE! But, we never have to go it ALONE! One of my goals to share with this book is that…YOU ARE NEVER ALONE! Life's journey can be beautiful, but it can be *oh-so-scary*! There are support systems everywhere! There are therapists, coaches and healers of all types for all purposes. I believe that other than my gift and destiny to be an Actress, I had to go through the experiences, challenges, trials, tribulations, accomplishments, wins and successes that I went through to discover my other "callings," as a Life Coach, Dating Coach and Dating Expert. Somehow, this feels right! Somehow, this all makes sense! I now understand how to use my HOT MESS to help and support others. I am perfectly imperfect and THAT is what makes my coaching, advice and tips so valuable.

Another valuable piece of advice is, "Follow the signs!" I have friends who are committed to following the signs from the *Universe* on a daily basis. I admire them for being so trusting of life and the *Universe*. I am not quite so trusting. But, over the years, I committed to a rule. If three different people shared information with me inside of a specific period of time, I would follow or explore it. So, when three people in my life suggested I compile all the information and writings I have worked so hard for the past several years, I felt compelled to do some serious soul searching. I had been so frustrated, overworked and underpaid, my stress levels were through the roof, my self-esteem was suffering and it was affecting my health again.

I sat and coached myself around it and tried to discover what was at the core of my frustration. I discussed it with my Life Coach, Lori Bertazzon, in our next session. As a Life and Dating Coach, I have been fortunate and grateful to have had my articles and advice published in many prestigious publications, and shared my wisdom and talents on several morning shows, talk shows and telesummits. I was the proud Co-host of the talk show *Breaking Dating* that aired every Thursday night and in January 2016, I earned the title of *Tempted. com Dating Expert & Spokesperson*. I want to be clear and state again how blessed and grateful I feel to have had these amazing opportunities! But...my frustration stemmed from feeling scattered and like I had not accomplished anything of my OWN! I felt scattered working for so many different companies and sites and seeing my work scattered across so many places and platforms. I watched clips from the TV shows, that I busted my butt to prepare for, archived on the internet and links from brilliant 2,000 word articles I had proudly written, disappear online a year later. I spent days and nights writing articles for way below my pay rate, and some even for free. I wrote, produced and created shows and content for other people's companies and never felt respected or appreciated. My soul was in need of something for ME! And, something I could, in turn, share with YOU! As my wonderful friends and coaches said to me, "You give so much to others, your work and everything you do, wrap it in a bow and give it back to you!" I listened and it felt right! While preparing this book, I felt the frustration dissipate. For the first time in a long time, I was doing something for me. I was the BOSS of me (LOL)! I didn't have to answer to anyone, seek approval or receive edit changes. I could freely express myself and share what I choose. Oh, you better believe this book caused this HOT MESS plenty of stress and anxiety to write and structure (Virgo!), but for the first time in a long time, I felt FREE!

I have also felt a great sense of joy and accomplishment writing this and I only hope that something I share on the pages to come, helps, supports or inspires you in some way. There is something valuable in these pages for everyone. You will find advice and tips for

Life, Love, Female Empowerment, LGBT Support, Self-esteem, Body Image, Bullying, Ageism, Dating and Online Dating. If one thing I coach helps you, this was worth all the frustration. If you only read one chapter that speaks to you, this was worth it. If you keep this book on your bedside table to turn to when you need a tip or reminder, this was worth it. If you learn to love your body, no matter what number is on the scale, this was worth it. If you learn to face your fears, this was worth it. If you feel compelled to get back out there and date after a breakup or divorce, this was worth it. If you choose to try online dating, this was worth it. If you learn to honor yourself and your choices, no matter what (flaws and all!), this was worth it. And, last, but not least, if you accept coaching and advice from a professed HOT MESS, this was so worth it!

HOLIDAY TIPS

HOLIDAYS ARE A festive and fun time to gather with family and friends, but also a fabulous time to touch base with ourselves and take stock of what we have to be grateful for or the changes we want to fearlessly make. I have been invited to write articles for many publications at holiday time, since readers tend to take a day or two off from their busy lives and schedules and fill their days with love and people they care for. Whether looking for tips for a red hot Valentine's Day or how to face your fears at Halloween, these holiday coaching tips can be followed any day of the year!

TIPS FROM A SCREAM QUEEN TO AVOID SCARY DATES ON VALENTINE'S DAY

When not executed properly, one of the most fun, loving, romantic nights of the year can quickly turn into a Scream Queen's worst horror movie! As a single woman and horror actress, I have experienced my share of real life scary dates on Valentine's Day! Here are some quick and fearless tips, so you can avoid the urge to shoot an arrow through your date…literally (LOL)!

PLAN AHEAD/IN ADVANCE

Whether making a dinner reservation, buying tickets to a show or ordering flowers, the worst thing you can do is wait until the last minute. Trust me when I tell you that most events on Valentine's Day night will have been booked weeks in advance. I remember one year, I was dating a guy and the relationship was fairly new. He invited me out to dinner, but neglected to make a reservation. You cannot get a dinner reservation on a regular night in Hollywood, let alone on Valentine's Day! Needless to say, we ended up driving around, stopping at six different restaurants and finally landed a meal at 11PM! Let me just say, I can be quite scary when I am starving (LOL)! By taking the time to plan ahead, you will show your date how much thought you put into the night and how special you think he/she is!

KNOW YOUR DATE

It is very important to be mindful of your date's specific needs and interests, before purchasing a gift or making plans. If your date is allergic to flowers, Valentine roses may not be your best bet! If your date has a seafood allergy, I suggest skipping *The Lobster* (unless, of course, you want your date to look like *Hitch* at the end of the night!). Also, Guys (and, this is a big one!), do NOT buy your girlfriend sexy lingerie in a size small, if she is actually a size large! You will end up crushing her self-esteem, rather than making her feel sexy! I remember the year one Ex-boyfriend planned a "very romantic" weekend away, then surprised me with a ghetto motel in Rosarito and beer games at *Papa's & Beer*. Needless to say, I was single again after that Valentine's Day! Show your partner love and respect by knowing his/her likes, dislikes and requirements.

DON'T OVERDO IT!

I have experienced and witnessed people spend WAY too much money and romance on Valentine's Day. Often times when a relationship is new, people want to impress each other. Now, we know that I am all for a man courting a woman and romancing her, but don't overdo it! Ladies, this goes for you too! There is a time and place for expensive gifts in a relationship and you want to give them for the right reasons. I have seen women gaga over a man and do extravagant things to keep him! This goes just the same for overdoing the romance of the night. You do not want to create a setting or emotions that are not REAL and don't really exist. I remember one guy I dated for a month and was on the fence about continuing. He planned the most romantic Valentine's date by hiring a private chef to his home, having rose petals sprinkled from the driveway throughout the house, candles everywhere, gifts planted all over and, sadly, I...*was just not that into him*! I felt very uncomfortable and stopped dating him shortly after. My advice is to keep it REAL, give whatever you give from the heart and, remember that it really is the thought that counts!

DON'T EXPECT/HAVE EXPECTATIONS

This is another important tip I preach to both men and women. People tend to have too many expectations on Valentine's Day and can become quickly disappointed. Women, especially, tend to create stories in their heads of what they "think" Valentine's Day should bring. I have had many clients come in for a coaching session after this holiday (birthdays, too!), crying or screaming about how their boyfriend of two years did not propose. I have also had clients come in frustrated about how the guy they have been dating for two months did not ask them for an exclusive committed relationship. I have even had more female clients come in devastated that their boyfriend did not buy them some fancy piece of jewelry or diamond earrings. And, a big male client complaint is that they took a woman out for a romantic third date on Valentine's Day and she did NOT have SEX with him! Sorry, Guys, you should not have "expected" that one! There is no need to add pressure to a day that is supposed to be filled with love and joy. Be in the moment, enjoy whatever the experience brings and I bet you will not be disappointed!

Don't Compare Yourself Or Your Date/Spouse To Others/Others' Dates

This tip applies to Valentine's Day, but I think it is important to follow it in our lives and relationships every day! Every person and relationship is different and unique. It is very easy (and, normal!) to get caught up in comparing ourselves and our partners to others. It is never easy to sit next to that "wealthier" couple at dinner, watch the man present his woman with the diamond earrings you have been dreaming of, then step into their limo. Or, be the only single person at your friend's Valentine's dinner party. I remember a friend calling me in tears once on Valentine's Day, because her husband did not plan anything romantic, while another friend of ours' husband surprised her with a trip to Maui. I also remember one Valentine's Day when I opted to pass on a date and go to dinner with three other single girlfriends. It was not easy to watch all the couples holding hands and kissing at the restaurant. For a few brief moments, I thought, "There must be something *wrong* with me." But, for all the single ladies reading this, the truth is, I have had some of the greatest holidays ever with my other single girls! And, I have also been blessed with men courting and romancing me on Valentine's Day, in ways I could never have imagined! So, before you compare yourself, partner or date to another, be grateful for all the love you have in your life on Valentine's Day and every day!

6 TIPS FOR A RED HOT VALENTINE'S DAY

One of the best things about being a single woman who dates a lot is that I have been fortunate enough to experience many hot dates on Valentine's Day, birthdays and beyond. When recently asked on a TV morning show for ideas for Valentine's Day, I came up with these...**6 TIPS FOR A RED HOT VALENTINE'S DAY:**

A COUPLES' MASSAGE

When thinking back to past hot dates, two "touch" me immediately! I was dating a new guy and on our fifth date, we impulsively drove to Thai town in LA and he bought us a Couples' Massage. I remember lying next to one another and watching each other squirm in ecstasy, as we were being touched. I can picture the look in his eyes and it was HOT! We had a sexy night when we got home. One Valentine's Day, I surprised a serious Ex with a Couples' Massage at a high-end private massage spa. While one person is receiving a massage, the other is in a robe lounging on a couch drinking fabulous wine and snacking on French cheeses, cured meats and breads. When the single massages were through, the two of us were left to devour the delicious delights, including each other!

VEGAS BABY

Whenever I think of my hottest weekends away, nothing compares to my weekends in Vegas! You want to design a hot Valentine's weekend of debauchery for your significant other? Do it Vegas style! Whether it be a master suite with a Jacuzzi in the room or "gettin' busy" on a balcony, "What happens in Vegas, stays in Vegas", right? There are some of the most renowned restaurants for a magnificent meal, spirits being poured like soup and, Ladies, you can get away with your dress "all about that bass". Of course, they have my favorite *Agent Provocateur* at *Caesars* for an "awesome-saucy" nightcap!

HIT THE HUSTLER STORE

Raunchy, hot, sexy? Your partner won't know the difference (or care!) when it comes to love and sex on Valentine's Day! Hit the *Hustler* store and try on the sexiest, scantily clad costumes they supply and show off your goods to your partner. Then, stroll over to the DVD department and browse the covers. Purchase the hottest outfit and DVD that turned your partner on and race home to make your own hot sauce. Made with LOVE, of course!

GOOD OLE BUBBLY

I stand by my favorite "French Tickler" Champagne every time! Champagne has always had a hot and sexy vibe for me! All alcohol is a bit of an aphrodisiac, as it tends to lower our inhibitions and put us in the mood, but there is something about the bubbly that makes us tingle head to toe! Add strawberries to the mix and have your partner feed you, while sipping. You will be feeling as hot as Cleopatra in no time. And, for those on a budget or not a fan of Champagne, pick up a bottle of pretty Prosecco and pretend you are disrobing in Rome!

GODIVA CHOCOLATES

Listen, ALL chocolates turn us on, but there is something sooo "diva-like" about *Godiva* ("diva" in *Godiva*). Maybe the thought of knowing how much money someone spent on wetting my palate is a bit of a turn-on for me? As soon as I see that *Godiva* box, I start to feel the inner Goddess in me surface! Bringing out my inner Goddess or being made to feel like a Princess (or, Prince!) is a hot trigger for me!

A HOME-COOKED MEAL

I always say that it is easy to get my sexy going with a dinner at *Mastro's Steakhouse*, but...there is nothing HOTTER than a guy who cooks me a home-cooked meal! Taste does not even matter! The idea of someone slaving over a stove, taking the time to shop, prepare, cook and serve me is sooo hot! It is the thought that turns me on and I am in a place of massive "appreciation". When we are with people we appreciate, we love to show them our "appreciation" after dessert is done!

TIPS TO CREATE YOUR OWN 'LUCK IN LOVE' ON ST. PATRICK'S DAY

Being a festive and fun gal, I am all for spreading and attracting luck with green beer and a four-leaf clover, but you may have more power than you think over your 'LUCK IN LOVE' on St. Patrick's Day… and every day. Here are some tips, thoughts and visualizations to…**CREATE YOUR OWN 'LUCK IN LOVE' ON ST. PATRICK'S DAY.**

CHOOSE AND VISUALIZE IT

Our thoughts create our feelings, so *choose* and *think* your luck in love! *Visualize* the person and type of love you want. I mean really visualize it! Visualize every detail from the person's height to profession to charitable activities to the car he/she drives. Feel it! Feel the deep, warm feelings in your heart and tummy that it feels like when you are madly in love. Use the *Law Of Attraction* principles! Tell yourself how lucky you are to have found the "ONE"! And, most importantly, *believe it* and that you *deserve* to have it!

REPEAT THE PAST

Now, typically, you will hear me coach people to "leave the past in the past", but this is one of the exercises, in which the past is welcome! Think about some of the luckiest times in your love life and repeat the steps it took you to get there. Remember every moment and detail from the time you met that person to the behavior and choices you made along the way. Lay the foundation based on those past magical situations you found in love. Then once you have taken inventory, prepare to, once again, put those steps into practice and take action!

Luck By Association

Many experts will tell you that "you are the company you keep". If there is any truth to this, then you want to surround yourself with people who are lucky in love! Find people in your life who have had luck in either dating, relationships or marriage (whatever it is you are seeking), ask questions and observe. Really listen, as they share their love stories. Surround yourself with people in successful relationships. Associate with people who have what you want. Feel their love and joy and know that it can rub off on you, too. In fact, rub these people like you would a rabbit's foot! :)

Work For It

Sometimes we create our 'luck' in love with good old-fashioned hard work! Whether in dating, love or career, I have always been one of those people who chose to work hard! When things you want do not come so easily, you want to take serious action! Although possible, it is not likely that the "love of your life" will show up on your door step. I say to put yourself out there and join that online dating site. Try Speed Dating! Throw on your hottest and classiest outfit and head to that fancy hotel bar. Save your money for a singles trip or tour to Paris or Italy. Luck will come, because YOU put in the work and made it happen!

TIPS TO HONOR A MOTHER ON MOTHER'S DAY

Although, I chose not to have children of my own, I truly believe that motherhood is one of the most difficult jobs around. I have watched women tirelessly put their children before themselves, and, their needs, before their own. I have witnessed women hold full-time jobs, while raising three young kids and single Mothers playing the role of both parents. No parent is perfect and our Moms may have made some mistakes along the way, but a Mother's love should never be forgotten. So, follow these easy...**TIPS TO HONOR A MOTHER ON MOTHER'S DAY.**

PUT THE PAST IN THE PAST

Sure, we are all a little effed up from our childhood, aren't we (LOL)? So, on Mother's Day, choose to put the past in the past, live in the present and let go of the mistakes your Mother or your Sister made when you were growing up! Find forgiveness for anyone or anything you feel may have "wronged" you. Rather than allowing yourself to feel like that 12-year-old kid again, be an adult and come from a place of LOVE!

WORK WITHIN YOUR BUDGET

I know it is a big thing to take the family out to a Mother's Day brunch and get all fancy! Trust me when I tell you that your Mother or Wife will appreciate the simple and "real" gifts just as much, if you are on a budget. Think back to when you were a kid and you brought home arts and crafts that you made for your Mother at school. Her eyes would light up when you gave them to her, wouldn't they? Bake her her favorite cake, pie or brownies and decorate a gift box from scratch. Make a collage of photos of the family. Any woman will appreciate the effort you put into this. And, remember, you created it from your heart, so it is priceless!

Tell Her How Much You Love Her (In Person Or Via Phone Or Skype, Not Via Email Or Text!)

Communication is a lost art these days! Yes, cards are wonderful, but go that extra step and tell your Mother, Step-mother, Grandmother, Wife, Aunt, Girlfriend, Partner, Sister, Daughter, etc…how much you love her and give specific examples of all the things she does that you are grateful for! With families and friends living further apart than ever, it is even more important to express and show love for the people in our lives. If you are on different coasts or in different countries, set a *Skype* or *Facetime* date, so you can see the smile on the Mother's pretty face, when you tell her you love her!

Do Something Special For Someone Who Is Not Your Mother

Life can be challenging and lonely and a lot of people are facing hardships these days. Go out of your way and give a card or a flower to that neighbor who is a single Mother and always offers to drive your child to school. Maybe there is a Mother at your work whose children live in another state. Bring her a chocolate kiss and make her day. Visit a home for the elderly and spend the day with an elderly Mother/Grandmother/Great-grandmother whose family lives in another city. Keep her company and have her tell you stories about her children and grandchildren for a few hours. I am willing to wager that YOU will be the one filled with LOVE when you leave!

TIPS TO HONOR A FATHER ON FATHER'S DAY

Let's just admit right now that sometimes we forget to honor the Fathers in our lives. Often times, they are our caretakers, providers, protectors and we know we can always count on them. They pick us up when we fall. They come home, after a long day at work and help the kids with two hours of homework. They drive hours to see the kids on a Saturday, when they no longer live in the same home. They comfort us after a losing game or a broken heart. And, sometimes… they need to feel loved and comforted too! So, on this special holiday, here are some…**TIPS TO HONOR A FATHER ON FATHER'S DAY.**

ACKNOWLEDGE YOUR FATHER FOR ALL HIS HARD WORK

After all these years, and being a Life Coach and Dating Coach, I still can't figure out men, but what I do know is that men need and love to be acknowledged for all they do, provide and work for! A man's self-worth is often based on his success and accomplishments. So, let your Father or man in your life know that you recognize and are grateful for all he has done to keep your family afloat and happy.

LADIES, LET YOUR HUSBAND OR 'BABY DADDY' KNOW WHAT A GOOD FATHER HE IS

A lot of women compliment their men on how romantic or thoughtful they are or how well they cleaned the house on Sunday, but they forget to let the men know how wonderful they are at fatherhood! We have all witnessed how fatherhood has changed many men's lives. Many men will tell you that their greatest accomplishment is their children. Men take pride in being a Dad and doing the best job they can. They deserve to hear that you think so too!

Plan Something Macho And Out Of The Ordinary

Ladies, yes, this is a day when you may have to kick off the *Louboutins* and play the role of a racecar driver! Whether it be fishing, hunting or hitting that baseball game (I'm more of an *Eagles* football gal, myself!), get guy-ish and take him out to the ballgame! Think about all the weekends Dad has spent taking your daughter to dance class or watching that Saturday night chick flick with you, so choose a fun day, event or activity he rarely gets to do and plan it! And, email us pictures of you playing paintball!

Pamper Your Father/Husband/Man

Tell Dad to take a load off! Bring him breakfast in bed, pop in whatever DVDs or *Netflix* he wants to watch all day, draw him a bath and play his favorite music! Pick up his favorite "cheat day" food from his favorite restaurants. Give him a full day without fixing anything or solving any problems. Make Father's Day all about him and he will feel like a King!

HAPPY HALLOWEEN! LEARN TO FACE YOUR FEARS

DON'T FIGHT YOUR FEARS...FACE AND EMBRACE THEM!

Halloween is one of my favorite holidays, so what better issue to discuss than fears? I mean, we all face them, right? As an actress who has worked on quite a few scary movies in my career, I have been faced with fears both on and off screen. In sharing openly and honestly with my lovely readers, fear is one of my greatest challenges in life and an issue I commit to working on every day! I find it fascinating that so many people think they are alone with their fears. I would like to dispel that thought by sharing with you that at some point in our lives, we are all challenged with fears around not being good enough, not being pretty enough, not being talented enough, not being smart enough, not being loved, taking risks, being broke, failure and maybe even success! Many of us drive ourselves "batty" (Halloween joke!) with the endless "chatter" in our heads about why we are afraid to live our lives fully and do the things we really want to do. Well, do not fret! Here are some tips to help you channel your fearless inner *Lady Gaga* and learn to face your fears!

CHANGE YOUR THOUGHTS

In my many years of metaphysical and spiritual studies, I have been repeatedly taught that *our thoughts create our feelings*! Our minds are really powerful! When we focus on negative thoughts, we start to feel a negative sensation throughout our hearts and bodies. Try it and see! So, when you start to think about your fears and focus on why you cannot or should not do something, change your thoughts, focus on and tell yourself all the reasons you can, should and *will* do it! How do you feel now?

Write It And R.I.P. It

Both personally and as a Life Coach, I am a big fan of journaling and writing stuff out! I believe it truly helps us to purge our negative feelings and frustrations. Take a piece of paper and write down all your fears and negative feelings around them. Be as brutally honest with yourself as you can be! Remember, no one will see this, but you. As you write them, you can also "scream" them out loud (Hey, it is Halloween and Scream Queen season!), as it may help you to get rid of them more powerfully. Once you feel that you have released all your fears, tear that piece of paper and those fears to shreds! Get rid of them and let em' R.I.P.

Fear Equals Act Anyway

Please allow me to be clear that this is easier said than done. I learned this concept in a "power of the mind" class many years ago and it stuck with me so strongly that I often use it in my coaching. We all face fears, so instead of fighting them or denying them, why not acknowledge and embrace them? Let's powerfully feel our fears, sit with them for a few moments, then act anyway! In other words, own your fears, smile and like *Nike...Just Do It*!

3 WAYS TO HAVE AN ATTITUDE OF GRATITUDE AT THANKSGIVING TIME

WE HAVE MORE TO BE THANKFUL FOR THAN WE THINK!

Thanksgiving is that time of year when we are reminded to take stock of all the wonderful things we have to be thankful for! Now, as much as I am committed to living my life with an "attitude of gratitude" all year long, let's be honest with ourselves and admit that some days we wake up in a funk, focus on the negative, worry about the things we *don't* have and simply feel sorry for ourselves! We are human and our feelings of gratitude can ebb and flow. Life is not always "easy" and can throw obstacles our way that challenge us at the core and make it difficult for us to be thankful. I believe that these are the times we most need to focus on the positive and realize what we do have to be thankful for! I mean, I was having a lousy day today, until I realized how lucky I am to be able to share my thoughts and feelings with you! So, *thank you*, in advance, for allowing me to share a few ways to help you have an "attitude of gratitude" this Thanksgiving!

TELL FIVE PEOPLE YOU ARE GRATEFUL FOR THEM

Okay, you *iPad* junkies! I will not deny you the pleasure of sending this via email, but, trust me when I tell you, the power and emotion behind seeing the person's face or hearing her voice on the phone will come back to you tenfold! So, tell five people that you are grateful for them and be very detailed in what you are grateful for. Speak from your heart and tell them how much they mean to you and why. You can choose anyone from your husband to your dog walker who gives *Fluffy* love, while you're at work! When you see how grateful these people are to be acknowledged, you will feel super grateful to have them in your life!

Choose A Charity Day

When you are feeling sorry for yourself, my first suggestion is to step outside yourself! There are always people facing challenges that are far worse than ours! I understand that this is all relative, but if we can walk away from our worries for a day, we often discover that we have more to be grateful for than we thought. For many years, I have supported women battling breast cancer and *Variety* children's charity and there is nothing more gratifying than empowering people to battle their way back to health! Spend a day at a homeless shelter or a senior center and truly share the love in your heart. You will feel grateful that you did!

Create A Thirty Day Gratitude Book

When a spiritual healer told me to do this years ago, I wasn't sure what the experience would be like for me. Well, it was incredible and I am now known to create a month long gratitude book about three times per year and use this exercise often in my coaching practice. So, grab an old journal or purchase a notebook and take a few minutes each day for thirty days and write *everything* you are grateful for! And, I mean everything! I write things from my family to my acting career to the fresh salad I had at lunch to my hardwood floors to my car transporting me to my radio interview. *Everything*, even down to the small things we forget to be thankful for! When I create this, I feel a shift in my energy, attitude and positive things seem to flow into my life. Remember, we get more of what we focus on, so let that be gratitude!

COACHING **2**

FEMALE EMPOWERMENT

AS A LIFE Coach, Dating Expert, Actress and single woman, you will hear my big mouth preach about female empowerment, quite often. I am committed to living a life of integrity and authenticity and do my damnedest not to judge others. I know I have been judged many times in my life and careers. I think I have allowed myself to feel disempowered at many points in my life, so I became passionate about speaking and writing about it for others...especially women! And, ladies, if you, too, are a HOT MESS...OWN IT! Whether challenged with the scale or media messing with your mind or heading in for surgery, this coaching advice will help to empower you.

FOLLOWING YOUR DREAMS IN 2016

As the New Year approaches, we are taught to focus on making resolutions. In this article, I'd like to ask you to focus on following your dreams instead. Dreams can grow, change or expand and the new year is the perfect time to create them, commit to them and bring them to fruition. I encourage you to play really big with your dreams in 2016! Take a chance, take a risk and make a list of things you never "dreamed" were possible before. Challenge yourself and allow others to challenge you. Do not allow others to squash your dreams, discourage you or tell you that you "can't". It is much easier to get caught up in the reasons why your dreams "can't" happen, than to realize how or why they can happen! I will not be the first or last person to tell you that "life isn't always easy", so take a deep breath, face your fears and focus on how and why your dreams can happen!

As much as I love the term "following your dreams", I am also a big fan of the term "facing your fears". I learned long ago in my spiritual studies that we cannot have love and fear in the same space. I believe with all my heart that our dreams are created from a space of love. Dreams are inspired by the things we love most, deep within our soul. Dreams are nurtured by that warm fuzzy feeling that makes us smile, laugh and sends tingles down our spine. If we allow our dreams to come from a space of fear, we are not free to play full out, love what we do and explore and enjoy the journey. By acknowledging and facing our fears, we will ACT ANYWAY and find the COURAGE to follow our dreams!

I love to observe the behavior of young children. Have you ever observed kids in action? They are FEARLESS! In my acting and producing career, I have always felt that the natural fearlessness is what makes a lot of young children wonderful actors. They are not yet consumed with the mind's endless "chatter" of what they are doing "wrong" or what they "should" be doing differently. They have yet to become jaded by life's challenges, disappointments or the criticism of others. Most importantly, they are not focused on what others think of them. They are free and fearless and believe that anything is possible and dreams can come true!

I'd like you to try a simple exercise with me: Sit quietly, close your eyes and just "be" for 5 minutes. "Be" with whatever feelings come up for you. Think about the dreams you would most like to come true in the new year and the dreams that INSPIRE you most. Do not let the little voice in your head tell you "No" or "That's silly, it'll never happen!" Do not judge or allow others to judge your dreams. Remember, you can dream anything and everything your heart desires!

Make your dreams come true in 2016!

Be You…And, Be Fearless!

FINDING WAYS TO NOT ALLOW THE SCALE TO DICTATE YOUR DAY

LET'S BEAT THE BATTLE OF BODY IMAGE AND FEEL BEAUTIFUL!

How many of you have allowed the scale to dictate your day and how you feel about yourself? I ask you to be honest with your answer, as I will share mine with you. As an Actress, Life Coach and Dating Coach, you would think I have a handle on this, but body image and self-esteem are issues I struggle with and commit to working on every day! As a voluptuous woman, I have battled those "few extra pounds" and body image, since childhood. I have been scale obsessed, since high school and have made it my priority every morning (I mean, we have to weigh ourselves even before our coffee, because every ounce less counts, right?). It was not until I turned thirty that I got clear on how much I was allowing the scale to dictate my day and how "good" or "worthy" I felt about myself. It is amazing how my self-esteem rises and falls with a three to five pound weight gain or loss! My heart breaks when I think about the negative thoughts and words that have entered my mind about my body. Do the words "fat", "flabby", "ugly", "disgusting" or "loser" resonate with any of you? Well, I am committed to ending this negativity! As a Life Coach to teen girls and women, I refuse to be a hypocrite with the work I practice! I want to share the positive and help you to find ways to not allow the scale to dictate your day!

CHOOSE IT

In my coaching, you will often hear me say, "Choose powerfully! There is a lot of power in our choices." I feel strongly that we can choose our thoughts powerfully. You have a choice to stand on that scale and allow the weight and number to dictate how you feel that day or you can choose to say, "I will not allow the number on this scale to define who I am and what I deserve on this lovely day!"

Choose to not give your power away to that scale, your weight or a number.

Compliment Yourself On Three Of Your Best Attributes

It has been scientifically proven that what we focus on persists! When we jump on that scale and are disappointed with the number, we tend to focus on the negative and put ourselves down. I want you to allow yourself to feel whatever it is you are feeling on that scale, but within one minute of stepping off and feeling the negative feelings, head to a mirror and compliment yourself on three of your best attributes! They can be physical or emotional. If you love your gorgeous eyes, focus on how gorgeous you feel they are! If you know you have a loving heart, focus on how loving your heart is toward others. I want you to focus on those three best attributes every time you feel negative body image throughout the day. And, you can change these attributes often, as we know you have many fabulous ones and deserve to acknowledge them!

Make A List Of Women You Admire

I love this exercise and practice it often! Make a list of women whom you admire or aspire to be like. You can list celebrities, political figures, Mother Teresa or your Mom…it is your list! Next to the names, list all of the qualities you admire about them. You will be surprised by how different their body types will be. You will also be moved by their internal qualities and accomplishments! For as much emphasis as we put on the external and appearance, this exercise will show you what is truly important and impressive to others, including yourself! And, know that the incredible qualities you see in these women, are simply a mirror of you!

5 EMPOWERING WAYS TO STOP MEN FROM AFFECTING OUR SELF-ESTEEM

LADIES, IF WE BUILD OUR OWN SELF-ESTEEM, MEN WILL FOLLOW!

Ladies, whether you are eighteen or forty-eight, single or married with children, does this conversation resonate with you? I have had several experiences that have caused me to get clear about my own self-esteem issues that are triggered by men and came up with some advice to help others. During a coaching session, I remember one teenage girl sharing that she had a huge crush on a guy at school and went shopping to buy a bunch of new clothes to impress him. At a recent seminar, a lovely actress in her late twenties shared how she felt she was putting so much into keeping her new fiancé happy that she was neglecting her acting career. Last week, a single girlfriend called me freaking out about a guy she met online dating who didn't call her for a third date, then proceeded to tell me what a loser she must be! Then, the other day, one of my best friends, who is a career woman with a great husband and two babies, cried that she was overwhelmed and frustrated that her husband was expecting so much from her and she felt she wasn't doing a good job of handling it all. Sound familiar?

RESPECT YOURSELF

Naturally, we want men to respect us (and, they should!). However, it is up to us to respect ourselves first! I coach about making powerful choices. Be aware and conscious of even the small choices you make throughout the day. Choose powerfully, authentically and respectfully! You are the only one who has to wake up with YOU in the morning!

BRING SOMETHING TO THE TABLE

Whether interviewing with a male boss for a new job, meeting a guy for a coffee date or attending a business dinner with your husband, have something to share that you feel good about! Find a hobby, learn about politics, watch Sunday football or study a current event that moves you! You will impress yourself, others and your self-esteem will soar!

DO NOT PERSONALIZE

If the guy at school didn't compliment you on your new outfit, the guy you met online dating didn't call for another date or your husband didn't watch the kids, while you tried to sleep in on Sunday, do not take it personally! I know this is easier said, than done, but you can be aware that this is not about you, but about him! Do not make yourself wrong or not good enough and don't make things mean something they don't!

DO NOT PANIC

I am the "Princess Of Panic"! As women, we tend to be more emotional, than logical. We often jump to conclusions with men. Most of us have done this at work when a boss doesn't acknowledge us, when a guy doesn't call or a husband comes home from work very late. We totally give our power away to men or the situation. We think the worst, then blame ourselves. This is not healthy for our self-esteem! I recommend taking ten deep breaths and getting zen and in control.

DO YOU

This is my favorite saying and I can't help myself..."DO YOU!" As women, we tend to give so much away, including our self-esteem! We base our self-esteem on what men think/speak of us at work, home or on that dating site. Sometimes, it is important to be slightly "selfish". Sometimes, we need to put ourselves and our happiness first. When you give to yourself and allow yourself to replenish, you have so much more to give to others and you will feel so much stronger inside. Make time to take that dance class, garden, paint, go shopping or anything that makes "your" heart sing! I hear your self-esteem reaching an octave higher already!

3 WAYS TO STOP THE MEDIA FROM MESSING WITH OUR MINDS

MIND OVER MEDIA!

Ladies, I am truly troubled right now! I mean like the kind of troubled that feels so negative in my heart that I know it is time to make an appointment with *my* life coach! You see, I just finished reading the latest issue of *Vanity Fair* and, as all five feet, 118 pounds of me sits at my desk typing with my eighties off-the-shoulder T-shirt, hair in a ponytail and a PMS pimple on my cheek, I am obsessing about the perfect photo I saw of Angelina Jolie and wondering, "Where did my genetics go wrong?". Okay, maybe I am exaggerating a little and I choose to take my own tips, but I know that we have all been there! I recently coached a teen client who came into our session crying, because she feels she is "chunky" and only wants to look like Rihanna in her latest music video. I had a girlfriend share at dinner that she never misses an episode of *"The Dr. Oz Show"* and she spent $900.00 on supplements and remedies that were suggested, inside of three weeks. Now, I love me some Mehmet, but not at the expense of a pair of *Louboutins*! Let's not forget the online dating advice book I read, which suggests that women over forty "lower their standards," because they are not as desirable to men as they were in their twenties and thirties (I couldn't make this up!). Don't turn off the TV just yet! I will tell you how to empower your "mind over media!"

DO NOT BUY INTO THE PROPAGANDA

Media is often created to make money! Media can be misleading and it is your responsibility to determine what is truly valuable to you! Do your due diligence before you buy into the propaganda of the latest skin cream that makes you look ten years younger overnight. Before you go under the knife to look like your favorite celebrity, make sure you research every phase of surgery, as it is never as "easy" as they say. My readers are too smart for that!

CHOOSE THE MEDIA THAT MAKES YOU FEEL GOOD

I would be lying if I told you I am not addicted to Reality TV! Early on, I would check out an episode of just about anything (Yes, even *"Bad Girls Club"*!). I quickly realized that I was not feeling good from most. I continued to watch the shows that spoke to my heart. I love watching people share their talents with the world, like on *"American Idol"*, *"So You Think You Can Dance"*, *"The Voice"* and *"The Glee Project"*. I have cried my eyes out with joy, because these shows inspire people to follow their dreams, no matter what their lives were like growing up or what they look like. I suggest putting down that "trashy" magazine and picking up an issue of *Oprah*. I guarantee you will feel better.

DO YOUR OWN PROFESSIONAL PHOTO SHOOT

Take it from a gal who has done a few in her time! I believe the greatest way to learn about something is to experience it yourself! I remember the first photo shoot I did as an actress years ago. I was astonished when I learned that it takes an army to make a celebrity look like they do in movies and magazines. You will learn that *nothing* is *real*! They add fake hair, lashes and booby tape, then make-up and lighting to cover every "flaw", while stylists are pinning your pants, then they airbrush and *Photoshop* every picture. My point is… our "picture perfect" celebrities that we long to look like, are just as "imperfect" as we are! And, no matter what you look like, you will *feel* like a Goddess when you are through!

FEARLESS HEALTH THOUGHTS

I am an Actress and a Board Certified Life Coach who has been challenged with health issues for many years. My life coaching company is called *Be You And Be Fearless Life Coach*, so I am committed to courage and being fearless for both my clients and myself. I am headed to the hospital again this week for a test that will require anesthesia, so I felt compelled to share my feelings around this experience. I have been feeling a bit anxious...maybe even panicked, so I chose to relax, center myself and discover what is really underneath this anxiety and worry. What deeper feelings, emotions and concerns are coming up for me? If you have ever gone under anesthesia, you have probably felt similar feelings. What triggers such thoughts of dread for us when we are going under, even for a simple procedure? What fears are we faced with when we think we might not wake up? How does this put life in perspective? Is there a way to have...
FEARLESS HEALTH THOUGHTS?

So, I am going in for a relatively simple procedure and I am thinking, "What is causing me to be so freaked out and think the worst? Is it my neurotic nature in general? Is it that I am such a control freak over my life? Is it that I have conditioned myself to think the worst, after many years of health challenges? Is it a form of protection to think the worst, so that I am prepared? Is it death that I fear the most or not living? Most importantly, why does it take a health crisis or going under anesthesia to really think about these things and get clear about my life and fears?" Oh, Wow! My therapist and Life Coach really have their work cut out for them this week, before my procedure (LOL)!

I just got off the phone with one of my best girlfriends from college. We discussed my procedure and the uneasy feelings I am having around it. The first thing she said was, "I totally understand! It's the worst feeling to feel completely out of control! When you are under anesthesia, you have no control over what the doctors are doing to you or if you will wake up and you have to trust that you are in good hands!" I thought she made a few really interesting points that I had not thought of. Is it a control issue? Is it a trust issue? These are two issues that I struggle with quite often! These are issues that my family, friends and clients struggle with quite often. The feeling of having no control is the reason I hate flying so much! As an Actress and Life Coach, I have flown a "million" times for work and appearances and, no matter, how many times I have gone into the sky, I have felt anxious every time! Think about it...each time we fly, we have to give up control to the airline, the plane and the pilots and trust that we are in good hands and they will get us to our destination safely! This is a challenge for a control freak like me! I am forced to let go and trust. And, come to think of it, every time I fly, it makes me think about my life and how precious it is and all the things I want and plan to do, if I land safely...kinda like I feel right now, thinking about going under anesthesia!

In lieu of sounding like a melodramatic actress (or, HOT MESS!), I am sharing my honest feelings that I have discovered and that I am not ready to leave this life, yet! Facing this procedure has made me think about all I want to do and accomplish. I know it sounds cliché, but there are so many things to do and people and places to see. I think I am less fearful of dying and more fearful of not living and living life to the fullest! I think about my future TV series I have committed my whole life to and the villa in Italy I have dreamed of and all the things I want to do to help change the world. I think about the choices I would make differently in my career, friendships and romantic relationships and how I would like to "sweat the small stuff" a lot less! Most importantly, I think about LOVE...for others and myself!

Speaking of LOVE, I am in love with Bravo's "The Real Housewives" franchise! I was watching an episode the other night and one of the women on the show was heading in for plastic surgery. She became very emotional in the doctor's office and shared her fears around how she has three young children and was terrified of not waking up and being there to watch them grow up. I completely understand her concern. Facing death made her think about how precious her life and family is. I feel myself thinking about my family back east that I am 3,000 miles away from and how much more time I wish I had to spend with them. I think about how much I want to be there for my parents when they grow old, because they have been there for me and given me so much. I think about watching my nephew and niece grow up, even if it is often via *Skype*! I think about how much I want to fall madly in love, get married and grow old with my soul mate and sit on a bench holding hands at 80. Oh, and, kissing and sipping wine together at our villa in Italy!

As I write this and explore and discover my fears and feelings with you, one profound thought comes to me, "Why does it take something fearful or life-threatening to search within and gain insight and perspective on life?" I would like to live every day of my life in love and gratitude for the people and things I have, than complaining about what I don't have. I would like to live every day of my life believing in, planning and preparing for all the wonderful people and things that the future will bring, instead of worrying, thinking the worst or expecting terrible things to happen, because negative things have happened in the past and I don't want to be disappointed again. It is best to learn from the past and not live in it. It is best to focus on and create a beautiful future. And, do you know what just occurred to me? If by some small chance, I do not wake up from my procedure this week, wouldn't it be so much more positive and powerful if I went under anesthesia thinking how wonderful my life has been and how much more wonderful my life will be when I awake? Wow! Although that is not an easy thought, it feels much more powerful and FEARLESS! Thank you for taking this journey of self-discovery with me and allowing me to share my...FEARLESS HEALTH THOUGHTS.

5 REASONS MEN DESIRE DIVORCE

As a Board Certified Life Coach, Dating Expert and forever single gal who has dated more than a woman "should" (LOL), I have had the experience of dating many divorced men. Out of my own curiosity and interest in learning about the "other" species (LOL), I have asked some deep questions about this very topic. The discoveries I made may hit-a-nerve in us women, but probably shouldn't surprise us.

WOMEN LET THEMSELVES GO PHYSICALLY

Men are visual creatures! They love to look at fast cars, football and short skirts! Too often, after years of marriage and having children, women stop trying to look sexy for their man. Whether a couple has been dating for three years or married for twenty, a man wants to look at his woman and feel like he won the prize. He wants to be excited and turned on and he wants to know that his woman takes pride in her own appearance, as well as being proud to show her off at his business dinner. Ladies, I am in no way telling you to strive for false "perfection", but you can still "sexy it up" for your man, even with the added "baby weight".

SEX STOPS

Men are WAY more simple than we think! Think back to the Caveman! In a way, I believe men reach adolescence and stay there (LOL)! Like the old cliché...they want FOOD and SEX! As time passes, sex sometimes becomes routine, boring or only initiated by the man and he soon loses interests...or has an affair! I have had clients and dates share time and time again how their marriages ended, because they were having sex once every three months the last few years and, even more, who were sleeping in separate bedrooms. Remember ladies, men need to feel sexually desired too!

WOMEN STOP STROKING THEIR HUSBAND'S EGO

Again, men are simple! They are, however, needier than we care to acknowledge. From an early age, a man wants to be the best, most handsome, make the most money, so he can be a "Superhero". When women stop complimenting and acknowledging men and start "nagging" or making them wrong, they often seek praise elsewhere. For some men, receiving praise from their wives is even more important than sex! Women want to remember to boost their husband's self-esteem and ego and remind them of how good they are at even the little things. Men want to know they are doing a great job at EVERYTHING they do. Ladies, it does not make us weak to acknowledge them!

WOMEN ARE HAVING MORE AFFAIRS THAN EVER

As I have dated more divorced men, I am shocked to learn how many men have caught their wives cheating on them! The last eight divorced men I have met or dated, have all shared situations with me about their cheating wives. I have coached a few clients who have tried to make their marriages work after the affair, but their egos and manhood were so diminished, they were not able to sustain the marriage. Women are living more freely and independently than ever and they are finding time and justification for stepping out on their marriages. Ladies, I realize men have been doing this since the Stone Age, but we might want to rise above and be the stronger "species".

MARRIED TOO YOUNG AND HAVE GROWN APART

I always say that I believe people shouldn't marry until about age 30. We hardly know who we are as individuals, let alone as a couple or counterpart. I genuinely believe that men seek their best friend in a life partner and when they marry young and grow into a different person, with different interests and goals, they need to move on. The things and people we are interested in often change as we do. I know couples who seemed to have everything in common at 23, then NOTHING in common 15 years later! Marriages also, sadly, end quite often when the husband finally accomplishes his career goals, success or financial success. We see far too many marriages end when the husband makes a lot of money, then wants to be free to be the "player" he never got to be in his 20s or he wakes up one day looking for a younger, "hotter" wife. Optimistically, I believe that once most of these men get the playing out of their system, they will seek their best friend and emotional equal to marry the second time around and FOREVER!

3 REASONS TO GET SEXY WITH THE LIGHTS ON

As a Coach and single woman, I often recite the old cliché, "Do as I say, not as I do!" Now, I have insecurities the size of Texas, so when I was challenged with this question as a Dating Expert, I chose to dig deep to find...**3 REASONS TO GET SEXY WITH THE LIGHTS ON.**

UNLEASH YOUR INNER VOYEUR

If there is one thing I have learned as a Dating Coach and Single Woman who has dated a lot, it is that EVERYONE has a little "sexy voyeur" in them! We know that men are visual creatures, but I have also learned that it can be an absolute turn-on for a woman to watch a man devour her beautiful body inch by inch! This makes for a fabulous foreplay buildup and can be more seductive than the actual act itself.

THE EYES ARE THE WINDOW TO THE SOUL

This old cliché really does ring true! Whether we are at the beginning of a new and passionate sexual relationship and getting to know one another or we are madly in love and married to our soul mate, there is nothing more intimate and intense than connecting with the eyes! When you are in the throws of passion and the lights are shining, you can look deeply into your partner's eyes and know what he/she is thinking and feeling! This truly is what life, love and communication is really about!

KEEPING IT REAL

One of the biggest explanations and fears I hear from my clients (and, struggle with myself!) is, "I am too flawed to have sex with the lights on and he/she will discover my flaws!" I totally get it! When we get naked with the lights on, we are "exposed" in *every* way! We are not able to "hide" in the dark and this can be a very vulnerable experience! We are literally "stepping into the light" to reveal our scars from our breast reduction surgery or college football injury. We can no longer hide our cellulite or zits on our back and what does this reveal? We are *real and human!* We are all imperfect, but want to realize that we deserve to be loved (and, made love to!) regardless! I believe that this begins with self-love. I tell women all the time that the sexiest thing in the world to men (and, vice versa!) is *confidence*! When we are confident enough to strip down and do the deed with the lights on, we are stating that we love ourselves and are ready to share that love and get a little sexy! Let's just keep in mind that it is harder to "fake" it with the lights on, so better keep it "real"!

LGBT SUPPORT

AS SOMEONE WHO has always been unique and danced to the beat of her own drum, I have been drawn to the LGBT Community. Growing up in big cities and working in the entertainment industry, I have supported many of my gay and lesbian friends in "coming out," as easily as celebrating a friend's birthday. However, I learned that not all LGBT share these positive experiences. I have coached gay teens and witnessed what they have been put through with bullying and cyber-bullying. I may be heterosexual, but I have felt compelled and inspired to support the LGBT Community. I have spoken at several anti-bullying events and have written with a supportive voice for gay publications. I only hope that some piece of coaching advice I share on these pages helps to support the LGBT Community.

BE YOU…AND, BE FEARLESS!

I am an Actress and Life Coach with a mission! Okay, so maybe I am also a "drama queen" and "hot mess" with a powerful message. Do you know how many young people in the LGBT Community struggle with the courage to make the right choices and find their own voice? My mission is to empower young people in the LGBT Community to be courageous, so they can make the right choices and find their own voice. I am here to support you, guide you and honor you in areas where you are feeling stuck, confused, fearful, insecure or simply needing help. I am here to share some of my feelings and experiences, so that you understand how important it is to find strength and courage, even during challenging times. I believe that sharing and communicating is super important, because when you share, you learn that you are never alone. There are always people out there who have been through what you are going through. There are always others who are feeling exactly what you are feeling. Yup, I, too, have more issues than *The Advocate* and *OUT Magazine*! I, too, am still learning, growing and changing all the time. So, it is a joy to share the information I know and am still figuring out with you "gorgeous" (both inside and out!) readers. It is a joy to encourage you to **BE YOU…AND, BE FEARLESS!**

Now, you may be wondering how a big-haired actress from Philly/Jersey/New York qualifies to be an advocate and supporter of the young LGBT Community. Well, I have helped more friends "come out" over the years, than the sun comes out in La La Land! Really! Maybe they have chosen me, because I have always been a fabulous cheerleader with innate gifts of love, compassion and the ability to not judge or make people wrong for their choices. Or, maybe they have chosen me, because I have always been a bit "different" and danced to the beat of my own drum. Maybe it was because I have stayed true to my heart, soul, convictions and dreams, even when others have not approved. That said, my life hasn't always been easy. I have often felt like I don't belong. I have often felt like I am not "good enough". I have often felt like people don't approve of my choices or I am letting them down. I have spent a lot of time and energy caring too much about what others think of me. And, in more recent years, as my acting career put me into the public eye, I have been totally trashed on the internet (Don't even think about it, *Queerty*!). However, even in the face of judgment and disapproval, I have chosen to be FEARLESS!

Being YOU is a choice! Being FEARLESS is a choice! I love the statement, "With every choice, there is a consequence." Think about it. When we hear the word "consequence", we perceive it as negative. The actual definition of the word "consequence" is "a result or effect of an action or condition". When you read that, it no longer sounds negative, right? It is simply the result or effect of a choice you make, whether positive or negative. When I first heard that statement, I thought, "Wow! So, with every choice I make, there is a consequence...right or wrong...good or bad! With every choice I make, there will be a result. And, if a "consequence" can be right or wrong or good or bad, then my choices really are more powerful than I ever realized! Like, I actually have some power in what happens in my life. Now, that feels powerful!" So, being YOU, and I mean the true, authentic, real, living-out-loud YOU, is a POWERFUL and FEARLESS choice!

I believe this was always the message in my mission, long before I was a certified Life Coach, an actress in the public eye getting trashed on the internet or even living in La La Land (and, you should have seen how big my hair was back then!). I believe I have always been a supporter of others being true to who they really are, loving who they really are and finding their VOICE to let the rest of the world know it! Whether it was helping my smokin' hot sorority sister "come out" in college in Philly or helping my dear friend and Co-star of *Tony n' Tina's Wedding* Off-Broadway "come out" to his big Italian family in New York or helping my boy crazy writing partner "come out" and tell our other writing partners she was marrying another woman in LA, my message and mission remained the same..."BE YOU...AND,

BE FEARLESS!"

This message and mission later carried over into my passion project TV pilot/web series *Ms. Vampy's Tween Tawk, Teen Tawk & In Between Tawk* for tween and teen girls that I created in 2011. I wanted to create a show with positive messages about body image, self-esteem, facing your fears and following your dreams, while also discussing heavier issues like stereotypes, bullying and putting down other people. The response to the show was tremendous and I was grateful for the number of emails I received from the young LGBT Community. I remember one email I received that both moved me and broke my heart! The father of a 19-year-old girl emailed telling me how much his daughter loves *Ms. Vampy* and shared her story of how she came out to her mother and she tied her up and physically abused her. He wondered if I would email his daughter and give her words of encouragement. I emailed immediately, letting her know that she is not alone, that there is nothing WRONG with her and how COURAGEOUS she was for being true to herself. She was so thankful for my support and the support of her father. I wish I could personally reach out to every young person who experiences an awful situation like this, but maybe something I have written or said on my show will reach the masses. Hopefully, it will be *Ms. Vampy's* catchphrase: "When faced with fear, dig deep inside, find your inner "vamp" and Vamp It Out!"

Speaking of reaching out and sharing, I was recently lucky enough to connect with one of my longtime favorite, multi-talented actor/ singers Jai Rodriguez (Yup...you got me! I have been in love with him since *RENT* and I am a total Renthead!). I asked him, "WHOM and WHAT gave you the courage to "come out" at a young age and BE YOU...AND, BE FEARLESS?" Here is what he had to share:

"Even though I was "out" to some friends and family at 18 when I was playing Angel in *RENT*, it wasn't until *Queer Eye* hit airways that I was fully OUT. I was nervous and concerned to be attached to a project with the word queer in it. But after I started seeing the word and myself as the true definition (deviating from the expected) I embraced it. Coming out is a personal decision but know there are people who will love and support you in your road to accepting and owning who you truly are." -Jai Rodriguez (*Queer Eye, Gigantic*)

The adorable star of Showtime's *The Real L Word: Los Angeles*, Romi Klinger, was a doll to answer my question, as well:

"My mother gave me the courage and strength to come out and be me. Whatever me is. My mom was married to a woman and they raised me to be open-minded and love whoever my heart wanted. Man or Woman, as long as they treat me right. I thank my mom for my fierce attitude about love. Love should never be judged." -Romi Klinger (Showtime's *The Real L Word*)

Life can be challenging and you have one life to live! Be true to yourself and make powerful choices. Don't allow others to make you wrong for being who you are. Find the courage to express yourself and have a voice! When you feel stuck or fearful, reach out to people who encourage and support you. Always remember that you are never alone. And, every day, remind yourself at least once to…"BE YOU…AND, BE FEARLESS!"

AGEISM AND HETEROSEXISM IN HOLLYWOOD

I am effin' pissed! Okay, so this probably isn't a great emotion to be carrying around as a Life Coach! But, as an actress, I'm pissed! Why, you ask? Well, a month ago, my talent manager called to tell me they found the "perfect" role for me in a new TV pilot, listed in the breakdowns. The character was a comedic 30-something, petite, big-haired Jersey girl with a sassy, snarky attitude and an East Coast accent…um…DUH! I was sooo excited, because these roles are few and far between and they scream my name! My manager told me that the entire office was pitching me to the casting director to get me an audition. The following day, my manager called me again (she was about as pissed as I am now!) to tell me that they had worked all day and tried everything they could, but the casting director and producers thought I looked too young and would not see me for the pilot! Now, if you are going to get rejected from an acting job, you definitely want to hear that you look too young or too pretty, yet, the rejection was frustrating just the same! I mean, how could I look too young to be a 30-something Jersey girl? Go on…you are free to laugh! The explanation seemed ridiculous and tough to comprehend. Then, a few days ago, my manager pitched me to a film casting director for the role of a 25 to 30-year-old long, dark haired prostitute and the casting director told her I looked a bit too "old" and mature for the role. WHAT??? Would someone please come up with better excuses in Hollywood? At that point, I was so annoyed and frustrated, I went to grab lunch at *The Abbey* with my friend Steven who happens to be gay. Thankfully, Steven is an actor friend, with whom I can vent and complain to about the industry. I shared my story and my "pissed-ness" about the ageism that takes place in the entertainment industry and he shared right back that he was recently passed on by the producers of a TV pilot, because they thought he read "a little too gay" for the part! This, of course, led us into a whole pow-wow session about…**AGEISM AND HETEROSEXISM IN HOLLYWOOD**.

Now, I might be a bit biased, because Steven is my friend, but, as a producer myself, I would surely cast Steven in any role he was right for, whether the character was gay or straight, because I think he is a very talented and diverse ACTOR! And, I am still not sure what the producers meant by he read "a little too gay" for the part. Does that mean he was a bit too soft-spoken with his read or too feminine or not macho enough in his delivery? I'm sorry, isn't it the director's job to give the actor adjustments or help him tap into the different sides of the character? Or, does it really mean that, because Steven is "out" as a gay actor (and, he is not a big name), the producers were not going to seriously consider him for a straight character? Steven shared a few stories with me and I was surprised by how often he actually deals with heterosexism in the entertainment industry. It seems as though he deals with it almost as much as I, and my actress friends, deal with ageism, sexism and the casting couch! Needless to say, after dissecting this "entertainment discrimination" over lunch, I left feeling bummed and frustrated.

Fortunately, I had a Theta Healing session with my a-mazing Theta Healer, Karen Abrams, late that afternoon (Oh, you thought that life coaches don't need their own coaches, healers, therapists and support systems? Are you kidding? We need them more than anyone! LOL!). I love my sessions with Karen, because she really releases what is underneath my negative thoughts and feelings and she happens to be a lesbian, so I knew she would understand the heterosexism thing that was bugging me. I had gone into the session feeling like a victim, but left with some powerful discoveries. Both Steven and I were allowing ourselves to be victims of the entertainment business. We were making the casting rejections mean that there is something "wrong" with us. I finally got back into my power and realized that...I AM WHO I AM! I am 30-something and I cannot change that. Steven is gay and he cannot change that. And, why would we want to? There is only one of ME and there is only one of HIM and there is only one of YOU! And, the same "reasons", "excuses", "explanations", etc... we were given about why we weren't "right" for the roles, will be the same "reasons" we will be PERFECT for different roles in the future! I got back into the space of focusing on gratitude and being grateful for even having a manager who pitches me. Oh, and did I happen to mention that I got passed on for a role, because they thought I looked too YOUNG? Now, my fabulous readers, THAT is something to be grateful for!

THE MAGIC OF MAMMA MIA!

I was recently invited to rock the red carpet on Opening Night of *"MAMMA MIA!"* at the *Pantages Theatre* in Hollywood, California. I was incredibly grateful for the invitation and tickets to Opening Night and you never have to twist my arm to get me to go to a Broadway musical (Okay, unless, it is *"CATS"*!). As I did a fabulous video interview with *GAY.TV* in the magnificent entranceway of the historic *Pantages Theatre*, I took in the experience and something occurred to me. I looked around at the packed theater and wondered how *"MAMMA MIA!"* could still draw such a huge crowd after "100" years? I took a second look and wondered why the show draws such a huge crowd of single women and gay men ...what is THE MAGIC OF *MAMMA MIA!*?

Now, this discovery should have occurred to me long ago, since my single Mom and all of her "sexy-over-50" single girlfriends became obsessed with *"MAMMA MIA!"* the movie! All along, I thought they were hot for Pierce Brosnan and Colin Firth, but it goes so much deeper than that! As I listened intently to the show, shook my booty to the ABBA score and observed the audience's reactions, I realized that the show represents LOVE, EMPOWERMENT, THE NONTRADITIONAL and FREEDOM OF EXPRESSION and TO BE WHO YOU ARE! I mean, we follow a story here, in which young Sophie invites three men, whom her free-spirited mother, Donna, slept with 21 years ago, to her wedding, in hopes of finding out which one is her father. In fact, my favorite line in both the show and movie is when Sophie says, "Mom, I don't care if you've slept with hundreds of men!"...GO DONNA! LOL! The real point I am trying to make is that Donna CHOSE to live her life fabulously, freely and with love and happiness for herself and Sophie. She didn't CHOOSE the "traditional family unit". She didn't "have" to marry Sophie's Dad. She lived her life the way she wanted to, raised a lovely daughter and did it all in a gorgeous Villa in Greece...um...GO DONNA!

Don't get me wrong, there is plenty of eye candy in this show for both men and women...lotsa hottie Greek boys in swim trunks! Plus, what human over 30 doesn't love to sing to *"Dancing Queen"* and *"Take A Chance On Me"*? But, again, I am all about dissecting the deeper meaning and attraction to this show. Being a hopeful romantic, I am forever inspired by the subject of LOVE. *"MAMMA MIA!"* really is all about LOVE! In fact, I just found a quote that I loved from the *"MAMMA MIA!"* movie page, "Finding what is truly in their hearts, many may discover the course of true love." Kinda confirms MY discovery, doesn't it? I mean, Donna loves Sophie; Sophie loves Donna; Donna loves her girls from Donna and the Dynamos; Donna loves all three men; All three men love Sophie and they don't even know her; Sophie and Sky love each other; And, at the end we find out that Harry loves Nigel! See, *"Love Is In The Air"*...wait, that's John Paul Young, not ABBA!

Okay, getting back to ABBA and the show at hand, there were other topics that really spoke to me...EMPOWERMENT and the NONTRADITIONAL. I remember the story that Donna shares about how she had to leave home "Because a "good Catholic girl" doesn't get pregnant without being married first." Donna chose her "nontraditional" lifestyle and raised Sophie on her own! How many people do you know who are raising children on their own today and doing as excellent of a parenting job, as the rest? I think it is very empowering for single women to see the lifestyle and relationship between Donna and Sophie. Donna did a fabulous job of raising Sophie without a Dad. I also watch my friends, who are gay or lesbian couples, raise their children in a "nontraditional" man/man/, woman/woman, mother/mother/, father/father family unit with more love and happiness than any "traditional" "mother/father" household. Again, the message here really is, *"All You Need Is Love"*...wait, that's The Beatles, not ABBA!

Okay, so before this little Renthead starts quoting lines from *"Seasons Of Love"* (definitely *RENT*, not ABBA!), I hope my discoveries and interpretations of the deeper meaning and attraction to *"MAMMA MIA!"* resonates with you too! Now, I did have a glass of wine before watching the show, but I'm pretty sure the Actress/Life Coach in me heard the subtext correctly. If you get a chance to see the show in the future, look for…THE MAGIC OF *MAMMA MIA!*

SO WHAT SPEAK OUT

As an Actress, Producer and, now, Life Coach, I have been blessed to travel the world and attend many wonderful events, premieres, film festivals and award shows. I have met some of the most creative, eccentric, impressive, inspiring and interesting people on the planet. I have met people who I will remember forever and some I'd like to forget! Then, on that rare occasion, I will meet someone who touches my soul and truly moves me, with what he/she is committed to in his/her life and work! I never know how this person will "show up" in my life. I don't know his/her gender, age, race, religion, sexual orientation or anything. I just know that he/she has moved me and my soul and I am supposed to know him/her for a period of time. I know you know this feeling and experience I am describing and I know you cherish these experiences as much as I do. I was recently lucky to win the *HONOLULU FILM AWARDS 2012 SILVER LEI AWARD for my "MS. VAMPY'S TWEEN TAWK, TEEN TAWK & IN BETWEEN TAWK"* TV Pilot/Talk show/Web series. *Ms. Vampy* has become a positive role model with positive messages for young women and the young LGBT Community. Like myself, *Ms. Vampy* is a Vampiress with a mission to help put a stop to bullying and putting others down. *Ms. Vampy* is a stand for courage and being fearless (sound familiar?). When I found out we won the award, I began tweeting about it. Now, ya never know who you might meet via *Twitter*, but I got lucky a second time, as I met the coolest 20-year-old student filmmaker ever! Alix Vander Vlugt won a *Honolulu Film Award*, as well, for his film *"SPEAK OUT"*. I went to his website and lo and behold, this young guy not only created a film about ANTI-BULLYING, but he created an entire freakin' organization against bullying! I mean, is this kid speaking my language or what? And, at 20? Now, I am truly inspired! So, I felt compelled to dedicate this article to my new buddy, Alix, his film and to introduce all of you to…SO WHAT SPEAK OUT!

I would love for my readers to get to know this amazing,

courageous young man and his organization, SPEAK OUT, like I had the good fortune of doing, so I chose to share a mini interview with you:

BROOKE: Who is Alix Vander Vlugt, Executive Director, SPEAK OUT?

ALIX: I am a mixed-bag artist. I am a 20-year-old award winning filmmaker, most recently winning at the *Honolulu Film Awards.* I wrapped up a year of film school in Montréal this past spring and am continuing my education at Sheridan Tech Institute in the Media Arts program. I am currently shooting a new production this summer. As an activist, I started a not for profit organization, SPEAK OUT, in response to the ongoing bullying issues I witnessed when I was 15 years old. I led the growth of the organization internationally and have worked with students, parents, communities and celebrities. Anchored by the national day of pink event, SPEAK OUT works to raise awareness, produce creative content, lobby government officials and provide a forum online to discuss issues. I am a *TD Scholarship* winner (2011), currently working as a technology strategist for the Toronto Dominion Bank. I utilize my free time by writing, playing hockey, baseball and shooting pool.

BROOKE: What is the mission of your organization SPEAK OUT?

ALIX: Since its formation, SPEAK OUT has been student driven to end bullying. We strive to raise awareness, strengthen communities and foster positive relationships with our network.

BROOKE: Can you describe SPEAK OUT for my readers?

ALIX: SPEAK OUT is a student run organization determined to put a stop to bullying. I founded SPEAK OUT in 2008 and the organization has grown from its grassroots in Guelph Ontario to challenging the globe to become a better place for everyone. SPEAK OUT doesn't compete with other anti-bullying campaigns and organizations, but instead works alongside them to strengthen our message. Each year SPEAK OUT hosts an annual Pink Shirt Event in April. SPEAK OUT has released a documentary, sponsored by the *Pepsi Refresh Project,* that is available for viewing online and for download. Information regarding the Pink Shirt Event is available in our EVENTS section of the page. In 2012, SPEAK OUT will begin its transformation in becoming an incorporated charity and will search for new student leaders to shape SPEAK OUT in a refreshed outlook.

BROOKE: How does SPEAK OUT support the LGBT Community?

ALIX: As an ally of the LGBT community, SPEAK OUT and myself are always pushing the fact that LGBT and straight youth do not have to accept an environment of hatred, fear, and disrespect in their communities and daily lives. Unfortunately, there are pockets of bigoted, closed minds who fail to realize the equality and rights of others and have certainly made it difficult for youth to express themselves as who they are. SPEAK OUT strives to make it aware that it should not be about waiting for things to get better, but to take an active stance on making it better. As a straight youth myself, I have experienced backlash for simply agreeing that gay rights are an important thing to fight for. It should not matter who you are or what you identify as, speaking out for change is as important as someone perfectly healthy looking for a cure for cancer. SPEAK OUT works hard to foster a positive environment where LGBT youth can openly share their stories and look for support. I regularly keep in contact with students who feel threatened or beat down and try to work with them to find a solution or some help. I am always inspired further when I get an email back saying how successful they have become, or how things started working out once they took an approach to end the bullying. It may never be perfect but we are trying our hardest. More and more people each day are opening their minds and realizing that we are stronger together.

My dearest readers, I am so proud to introduce you to my new friend and inspiration Alix Vander Vlugt and his powerful organization SPEAK OUT! I ask you to imagine what the world and the future would be like if more young people would ban together and put their time, energy, passion and creativity into more organizations, films and public forums that spread a message like SPEAK OUT? I imagine a world where people perceive that they and others are PERFECT just the way they are! Until then...SO WHAT SPEAK OUT!

DATING TIPS

AS A LIFE and Dating Coach whose mission is to empower women and men, and as a woman who has been on more first dates than I care to admit, I made one of my major career goals to guide and support singles through the challenges and joys of dating. Someone once told me that to be a true "Expert," you need 10,000 hours of experience and expertise in that field. Well, you can rest your pretty little heads, because, as I publish this book, I can confidently assure you that I am an "overqualified" Dating Expert (LOL)! Yes, you are receiving dating advice from quite the experienced dater...even a HOT MESS dater, at times! I OWN it! I have openly shared on several talk shows that I am not an Expert on "relationships", but I know EVERYTHING there is to know about DATING (LOL)! This coaching chapter shares some tips to support you with your dating experiences.

THE HOLLYWOOD DATING EXPERT

EXPERT SUMMARY

"Drama finds her in her life, love and work...and, she works through it fearlessly every time! Who better to date coach singles than a Board Certified Life Coach and Dating Expert who has been through "drama" in both her life and work? Award-winning actress, producer, writer and coach, Brooke Lewis, has lived her own soap opera as a single woman on a mission to always follow her heart and pursue her dreams. Dating "more than a woman should", facing many challenges and a lot of heartbreak along her way, she is here to help singles Be Fearless through whatever drama dating and love brings them."

People always ask what qualifies me as a "Dating Expert" and I can genuinely say that I am like the missing fifth friend on *Sex and the City*. Without question, I am a hybrid of Carrie and Samantha, yet I still hold a bit of Charlotte in my heart! I share and own that I have dated approximately 1,500 men and have gone on over 1,200 online dates in 15 years. Over those 15 years, I forced myself to go out on so many online dates, it became like a part-time job! Sooo...I chose to really make dating my part-time job! I mean, after all this, I am an "expert" now, right? I also enjoy the old saying, "Those who can't do, teach!" I have become fabulous at teaching/coaching women and men how NOT to make some of the mistakes I have made. Although, I am actually a fabulous "dater" and make a great date most of the time. Where I fail is in *relationships*! I totally OWN this too! Whenever they ask me on TV what makes me a good Relationship Expert, I reply, "No, I'm a great dating expert. I know nothing about healthy relationships!" Here is what I do know: that I can help others make powerful dating choices; that I can cheer and support others in their quest to "get back out there" and date after a bad break-up, divorce, catfish or any other experience; I can help singles take the right approach to dating, as there are different approaches (and, dating sites!)

for different people; I can encourage people to be fearless, as dating can be scary; and, like Charlotte, I still know and believe that there is love out there for me and everyone! I really do KNOW and BELIEVE this! You would think that after putting myself and my heart out there as much as I have, I would be bitter and jaded, but I am still (as my *Match.com* profile states!) *in love with love and romance*! I am a "hopeful romantic" who KNOWS and BELIEVES I have a mission to coach and support people in crossing the bridge from dating to love!

Now, in full disclosure and a bit of backstory, my life has never been easy! My parents were divorced when I was two (we know this factors into the way we relate to men!), I battled severe allergies, asthma and immune system issues (this will come up later in regards to dating!) and I was a very emotional child, so I threw myself into the arts (what a surprise!). I share this with you, because it greatly affects my dating life, choices I have made and where I am today. Four things I knew for sure by the age of 13 were that I could easily attract and seduce boys, I wanted to be a career woman, I wanted to be an actress and I did not want children! It sounds crazy, but as I grew into adulthood, none of the four changed! I am fully aware and take total responsibility for the fact that I have been laser focused on my careers and, although I have had a few wonderful long-term re-lationships over the years, I have held them second to being a career woman! Now in the theme of challenges and being fearless, I took off to New York City at 22 and worked my butt off at auditions to land the Off-Broadway mobster comedy *Tony n' Tina's Wedding*. I did seven shows a week for three years and was livin' large! I learned quick-ly that starring in a Broadway show has its perks, including attract-ing and dating tons of hot Broadway and soap opera stars! I mean, who wants a serious boyfriend, when you have that at 22? My career moved into TV and film, which brought me out to Hollywood and into the "scene". Again, being in my 20s and going to *Sundance* and Shane Black's Halloween parties every year, I hardly wanted to be in a serious relationship, when I could date and make-out with drunken hotties instead (I know, I'm like a guy!)! Don't get me wrong, I partied plenty, but I worked my butt off! I was completely committed and married to my career and after pounding the Hollywood pavement and having failed sitcom pilots and series, I became a producer to create an acting career for myself. Talk about time and commitment! I worked about 15 hours a day for several years and dated a ton, but forgot to have a relationship (Ooops!)! Then, I woke up one day and I was in my 30s, had Executive produced and starred in a few horror/thriller films and had the title "Scream Queen" bestowed upon me! Hmmm...Broadway actress, TV sitcom actress...Scream Queen? Okay, I will take it! So, I worked my butt off again to become a "famous" Scream Queen actress and quickly learned that in the age of the internet, being "famous" for anything has its perks! So, fan mail flew in and guys came out of the woodwork to take me on dates!

As the internet exploded, so did online dating and, how convenient for me, as I was traveling for films and autograph signings, I could also be accepting dates from my computer? You *know* I joined every online dating site I could find! Although this was before the *Tinders* and apps, the action was insane! I remember making three back to back *Starbucks* coffee dates on a Saturday afternoon. So, my life was beyond busy with being a famous Scream Queen, producing and dating! Of course, I still made my career my priority and since horror was a success for me, I created an Elvira-like character named *Ms. Vampy*. *Ms. Vampy* is a comedic Brooklyn Mobster Vampire with a heart of gold. She was well-received and went on to have a hit web series. And, just when I was at the peak of my success in 2009, the economy crashed, my investors pulled out of projects, internet piracy of indie films exploded and just as I shot *Ms. Vampy's Teen Tawk* pilot for teen girls, I lost everything and was forced to "revamp" (pun intended) my entire life and career. I was so inspired by my teen girls and giving them support and advice, I took off of acting for two years and went back to school to become a Board Certified Life Coach. Yet, again, another challenge! And, yet again, another commitment that took me away from putting time into a relationship...so I just casually dated like crazy, when I felt like making time! I launched my coaching company, *Be You And Be Fearless Life Coach*, January 2012 and initially started coaching issues around Empowerment for Women. I soon discovered that even when clients would come for a session on something awful that happened at work, it would quickly surface that they were more upset over a fight with their boyfriend or a date that went bad or how lonely they were not dating now. Of course, being the "dating queen", I had all the proper support and suggestions. I also learned that when I would go out on dates with guys I wasn't interested in after 10 minutes, I would start dating coaching them...and, they loved it! I actually got a few male clients from online dates going wrong! So, I realized that this was my specialty and the coaching niche I had to pursue.

So, I hit the ground running and became more obsessed than ever with online dating! At first I joined several sites again to do my due diligence for my new career, but soon got caught up in my dating "addiction" again. I mean, I could convince any broke screenwriter on *Plenty Of Fish* to come over and watch a movie on a lonely rainy night or have dinner at *Mastro's Steakhouse* seven nights a week with the invitations from *MillionaireMatch.com*. Like Samantha said on an episode of *Sex and the City*, "A girl's gotta eat!" This is all very fun and exciting, until it isn't anymore! I have had some incredible experiences and have made some really stupid mistakes! I have seriously acted the fool on a few dates and drank just one glass of wine too many on others! I am human! I have learned that I cannot date men with pets (the allergies and asthma I told you about!), nor men who want children (I am not having them!). I have learned that I cannot date men who do not respect my careers or my work ethic. I have learned that I don't have to be in my 20s or a tall, thin model to attract men and dates! I have learned so much about myself, dating and men. My dating experiences could fill volumes of books (and, will one day!). I am still on the market and dating and, believe it or not, I still LOVE dating! I still love the newness and excitement of a first date! I still love that first kiss! But, I am still single! In many ways, I have chosen everything that has led me to where I am right now. There is a lot of power in our choices! I now choose to put my Dating Expert career before relationships and I am okay with it! My goal now is to get a TV series as a Dating Expert and show the world that there is no shame in being a sexy, sassy, single career woman! Sure, I sometimes get lonely! Sure, I sometimes wish I had a partner in crime! Sure, I hate being the only single person at the dinner party! But, hey! I have lots of hot guys who I've dated over the years, and am now blessed to call "friends", to take as my date! Plus, I have the most wonderful, beautiful (inside and out!) single girlfriends to turn to when we are lonely on a Saturday night and they just LOVE spending hours talking to me about dating advice. I say it is a WIN WIN! So, all my sexy singles, I will toast to YOU and hope that the dating articles in this chapter INSPIRE single people everywhere to want to get out, have fun and DATE!

HOW NOT TO LET DATING AND REJECTION GET YOU DOWN

Dating in 2016 can be challenging! As a Life and Dating Coach whose mission is to empower women, and as a woman who has been on more first dates than I care to admit, here are some tips to empower you with your dating experiences:

BE YOURSELF AND OWN IT

The best advice I can give to women in the dating world is be yourself and own it...flaws and all! Whether you are 21 or 51, dating in college or newly divorced, a sexy skinny minnie or a voluptuous vixen, you have plenty of interesting qualities and experiences to bring to the table. Share your strengths and interests that you feel good about with your date. Women often struggle with either being too vulnerable or having too strong of an opinion on a date, but I believe you should allow both and be yourself. The "right" man will respect that you are who you are, your past helps to create the person you are today and that you have an opinion. And, remember, what one man views as a "flaw" of yours, the right man will find utterly "adorable"!

DO NOT JUDGE YOURSELF OR GIVE YOUR POWER AWAY

Dating is supposed to be a fun and positive experience, but when negative circumstances arise, our affection is not returned or we are rejected for a following date, it is easy for us to take it personally and feel like something is *wrong* with us. Do not judge yourself or analyze what is *wrong* with you! When we do not get attention, affection, love or validation from others, it is easy to feel like we are flawed, not good enough or allow it to affect our self-esteem. When we allow other people to dictate how we feel about ourselves, we give away our own true power. Do not give your power away to a date who does not appreciate the A-mazing person you are! I promise another date will be coming who totally gets what a special "catch" you are!

Visualize Your Perfect Date Exercise

When I am motivational speaking or coaching private clients, I find visualization exercises very helpful. If you have experienced a lousy date, rather than feeling discouraged and getting stuck in the negativity, I recommend trying this exercise: Sit quietly with your eyes closed for 5 minutes. Take 3 deep breaths to release any negative feelings you are experiencing from your date. Then, I want you to visualize your "perfect" man and your "perfect" date. Get super specific! See and feel EVERY detail as you would want it to be! Visualize what he looks like, what he says to you, what you look like together, where you are and even what that first magical kiss feels like! You get the picture! My bet is that you will have forgotten the negative feelings around that lousy date and your heart will be overflowing with love and joy! Makes your dating future look and feel brighter, doesn't it?

FALL-ING FOR DATING

For as long as I can remember, fall has been one of my favorite seasons. I do not know if it is because I am a September, Virgo baby or because Halloween is approaching or because it sort of feels like a new year is coming. I do know that fall is a time to say farewell to the warm, carefree, lazy summer and set new goals and dream new dreams. As women, we owe it to ourselves to be happy and fulfilled at every season, but there is something "autumn-licious" about "fall-ing for dating" this time of year!

MOVING FROM SUMMER FLING TO FALLING

As a Dating Coach and Expert, and a single woman myself, I know how much fun a summer dating fling can be! Summer is notorious for taking a holiday or vacation, weekend parties in the warm weather and being quite the social time all around. In general, we are more footloose and fancy free and that can lead to us Ladies kicking off our *Louboutins* in a sexy stranger's direction! All you readers who took that Paris getaway and ended up drinking too many bottles of that fabulous Bordeaux with that handsome stranger at the café know what I am talking about. And, some of you spent the summer at your cottage by the lake kissing the new neighbor under the stars. The challenge here is that summer flings tend to "fall" short of reality and expectations. Each person returns to his/her "real" life, work and routine and the seductive, spontaneous summer spark simmers down. And, if long-distance dating is involved, there is a whole other set of challenges that follows. This is the reason fall is a fantastic time to get serious about dating and seeking a real relationship. As the fall breeze blows, dating and love flows!

FALL IS A TIME FOR STRUCTURE, SCHEDULING AND DATING

September comes and you single gals are back to the work grind, while you single Moms are busy getting the kids off to school. Time is precious and a schedule must be put back into place. This is the time when we set our career goals, get back to the gym or yoga and powerfully choose what we do with our little free time. I tell clients and friends that this is the perfect time of year to get back to (or try!) online dating and make sure to schedule in fun date nights for yourself after a long work week or chauffeuring the kids around! I am a big proponent of happy hour dates! They are easy to plan and get to right from the office, can be a simple two hours of cocktails and fun and are perfect for a blind date or first time meeting an online date. It is easy to get caught up in work and the kids, but remember to take a few hours and allow someone to pamper you once a week (or more ;).

THE HOLIDAYS ARE COMING...THE HOLIDAYS ARE COMING!

Ladies, we have all been single at times and coupled at times for the holidays and, for the most part, it is twice the fun to be dating someone at the holiday season (Except for the year I broke up with an Ex, took myself to Cabo for five days and made-out with the hottest British man who could have been Hugh Grant's long lost brother! Okay, that is for another article! ;). Fall is the time to get that energy flowing to attract that sexy suitor to dress as Elizabeth Taylor and Richard Burton for Halloween, give thanks with at Thanksgiving, exchange gifts with at Christmas time and toast to on New Year's Eve! And, this does not happen overnight, so you've got work to do! Dating truly does take work and commitment and finding the right partner can be challenging, but if you get very clear on whom you seek, set your goal, put yourself out there and open your heart, I have a strong feeling your next summer may be sizzling with your significant other!

Lovely Ladies, a New Year's "cheers" to you and dating in September!

THE DELIGHT OF DATING DIVORCED MEN

As a Single Woman and Dating Expert, I have had a great deal of delightful experiences dating *divorced* men. Naturally as we grow *fabulously* older, women are going to meet many more divorced men than we did in our 20s. Although there are still stigmas surrounding dating divorced men, here are a few reasons you will have a delightful experience.

MEN WANT TO MAKE THINGS RIGHT

Ladies, we all know that men are, by nature, *fixers* and *problem solvers*. Whether repairing the kitchen table or planning a romantic evening, the male ego and inner child has a strong need and desire to get it right and succeed. Men often feel this need after a failed marriage and while entering into a new relationship. I have witnessed this many times and men have openly shared with me that they would love to be married again one day and "make it right this time". I have dated divorced men who have acknowledged that they spent a great deal of time building their businesses during their marriages and they wish they had been more romantic or listened more or had brought their wives flowers more often or had been more complimentary to their women. Well, ladies, guess who benefits from those lessons? Yes, we do. There are many divorced men out there whom have taken the time to work on themselves and their *mistakes* or *shortcomings* after their marriage ended and they are committed to making things right the next time around.

DIVORCED MEN ARE ALREADY TRAINED

Ladies, as much as we love men (and, I really do!), we want to acknowledge that they do mature, grow up and learn a bit more slowly than we women do. I believe that marriage teaches men responsibility, structure, how to co-define reality, what women want and how to put someone else before themselves. I have giggled to myself and so very much appreciated the little things that divorced men I have dated have done for me. They have taken out my garbage, carried my luggage, taken my car for an oil change, cooked me dinner and brought me breakfast in bed. I have found that men who have been married are a bit more structured and trained to do the little things. They seem to naturally have more of a routine and offer to do things that a lot of men who have never been married would not think to do for another person. I have dated many single 40-year-old men men who are super set in their ways, while men who were married before seem to have a deeper understanding of taking care of a woman...in many ways.

DIVORCED MEN OFTEN HAVE CHILDREN

Ladies, I share very openly that I have chosen my career first and never wanted my own children. I have many single girlfriends who share this choice and many who chose marriage, had children and got divorced. I have found dating divorced men with children to be an amazing experience for myself, and my friends and clients who are now single women with children of their own. In my 20s, almost all of my relationships failed because I chose not to have children of my own. I understood and respected the fact that most men wanted children. As I have gotten older, I have loved dating divorced men with kids, because it has taken the pressure off of me to have children with them. I have also learned that men with kids love *that much more deeply*. I have completely fallen for a guy or two, simply by watching him with his kids and the undying love and support he has provided them. I have felt this love carry over to me, as well. These men seem to love much more unconditionally. For all you single Mom readers, I think dating divorced men with children is a huge plus. Men with kids will understand your schedule, lifestyle, priorities and responsibilities, because they will have a similar life experience. So, just imagine this single ladies...whether you are flying solo like me and gain a beautiful built-in family or you are a single Mom yourself and gain your very own *Brady Bunch*, you are gaining a wonderful experience by dating a divorced man who brings a lot to your table.

TIPS FOR MEN ON WOMEN WHO PLAY HARD TO GET

As a Single Woman and Dating Expert, you will often hear me quote, "Don't hate the player, hate the game." And, as much as men and women hate to admit it, there is *always a game* in the *Game Of Love*. I know, because I have played many and have prided myself on being *hard to get*. I also know, because some of my games have worked and others have shamefully backfired. So, Guys, take a few expert advice tips from a Lady who has been there.

Make Sure She Is Genuinely Playing Hard To Get And Not Super Busy

I know, we all hate the busy word. And, yes, we can choose to perceive it as an excuse, but I can tell you, firsthand, that I have been accused of playing hard to get or intentionally not being available when, in fact, I have been working 15 hour days. If I am speaking at an event or filming on set for 12 hours straight, I am not playing hard to get, but genuinely may not even have my phone to call or text you back, and I certainly don't have time to see you for dinner that night. Guys, like you, women are busier than ever. More and more women are uber focused on their careers. They are traveling for work and some are working more than one job to stay afloat. Divorce rates are higher than ever, so it is likely you are also meeting single Moms who are responsible for their children first. If any of you are single Dads, then you know that priorities shift when you have children. Some of these women will be both career women and single Moms, at which they will truly be challenged with time to date you. Now, Guys, I want to be clear, this does not mean that we don't *want* to spend time with you, but that we really don't have it to give you right now. Give it time, pay attention and feel it out. You will know quickly which woman is playing and which is truly busy, but is really into you and will make an effort to see you as soon as she can.

STOP ASKING WOMEN OUT LAST MINUTE AND START MAKING PLANS

Guys, this is one of my personal pet peeves. I am a rules girl and I choose not to accept a date the night of and, quite frankly, often not past Thursday morning for a weekend date. Now, there are always exceptions and last minute fun events or basketball tickets that come up, but we are focusing here on the beginning stages of dating, so humor me. My girlfriends and I have talked this topic to death and we have all said no to last minute dates and, of course, been accused of playing hard to get for it. And, believe me, it is not always easy and I have had to have serious self-control to say *no* to that sexy man who I had the hots for on the other end of the phone. But, remember, we teach people how to treat us. Guys, women want to be courted and made to feel special. They don't want to feel like a last minute plan or an afterthought. This may present itself as a game, but if you guys would plan ahead more and ask women out in advance, I'll bet you hear a lot more yes's and feel like women are a lot less hard to get.

IF A WOMAN IS REALLY PLAYING HARD TO GET, IT IS OKAY TO PLAY BACK A LITTLE

We all know that there is often a power struggle in the game of love. It really is like a basketball game and the ball bounces from your court to her court at different times, especially at the beginning when you are learning about one another. I am definitely guilty of having a guy pursue and chase me and make it oh-so-easy early on that I have felt like I didn't have to work as hard to build something and have, unconsciously or unintentionally, taken him/it for granted. Then all of a sudden...BAM! That curveball comes. He skips calling me for a day or two or doesn't ask me out for Saturday night and I go "cray cray". It happened to me recently and I can laugh about it now, but at the time was really freaked out, because he had been very consistent for the first month, then the curveball. He knew what he was doing and I have to give him props for playing the game. The ball bounced back to his court and I ran to get it. Now, Guys, let me be clear, I am not saying to do anything spiteful or hurtful or run and hook up with other chicks, if you are dating someone and into her. I am just saying that you are allowed to play hard to get once in a while too and she just may run right to you, rather than away from you, next time you see her.

Since I am an online dating *veteran*, I had to save two tips for that:

IF YOU MET HER ONLINE, STOP EMAILING AND TEXTING AND PICK UP THE PHONE

This is another huge issue and conversation amongst my female friends and clients. When you meet a woman online, remember, you have never spoken nor seen each other in person yet! I am old school. I need to hear a guy's voice, get a vibe and have some sense of his personality before choosing to meet. I have been labeled *playing hard to get or difficult* with many online dating prospects, because I have made a very clear choice not to meet a guy without a cool phone convo first. In this crazy and fast-paced age of technology, we have lost sight of quality, real intimacy and conversation. Fortunately, and unfortunately, we have options of people to date online, beyond anything we have imagined. I cannot tell you how many men I have clicked with via email online dating, then they asked for my number and I asked them to call me and, instead, have received a text with the expectation of having a full personal get to know each other convo via text messages. I have declined and requested a *phone call* every time. Some men have respected my request and others have labeled me tough or hard to get. Sadly, I bet I have missed out on a few good guys who just don't give good phone, but I'm willing to take my chances and hold out for the really good guys who want to make the effort to know me. Speaking of games, I actually have a guy who has been texting me for four months and we have never met. He will never call and I rarely respond and I think it has become a game to him to see how hard to get I really am. Funny, huh? I will retire my online dating jersey before I will go out with him.

If You Met Online, Hit It Off And She Is Still Online Dating All The Time, She May Be Impossible To Get And You Need To Walk

Guys, this is a tough one and I have had a lot of time and experience to think about it. We really do need to pay attention to timing, as *timing is everything*, but we also want to pay attention to behavior. I have had a lot of friends (male and female) and clients talk to me about how they met someone online, hit it off, even slept together and they see the person still on the dating site and feel they may be playing hard to get. In some cases, this is true and others, it is not and you need to learn the difference. Online dating has become like *Ebay*. The store is open and you can order any time and as many items as you'd like. You may have spent a romantic weekend in Napa with a woman, then caught her "online now" Monday morning. This is the nature of the online dating beast. She may genuinely want to date around and keep her options open at this time. She may be newly divorced or fresh out of a relationship and not looking to date just one guy. This does not mean she is not into you; it simply means the timing is off. You may perceive her as playing hard to get, while she actually is impossible to get at this time. I will end with a personal opposite story for you guys to relate to. I really hit it off with a guy online and really liked him. We dated for a month and were hot and heavy very quickly. Everything was awesome…except we were both still playing on that dating site daily. He let me know he saw me on there a few times and I made a few snarky remarks about him always being on there. This became an issue for us both and instead of being the bigger person and communicating with him, I played games and hard to get and would intentionally log onto the site and leave it open just so he would see me on there and I could light a fire under his ass. Well, as most of you have guessed, my games backfired and he told me he did not want to date a woman who was always online seeking other men. So, by playing hard to get, I lost a guy I was really into. I share that information in my last tip, so that maybe you won't make the same mistake, you'll communicate better and know when to walk away or try to make it work.

Guys, I never said the *Dating Game* was easy or that you will always *win*, but that *hard to get* gal might just be worth going after.

DATING AND FINE DINING

I am about to share some information with all you readers that you may not know. Other than being a Dating Expert, I have often been labeled a Lifestyle Expert. What qualifies me, you ask? I have been known to be a foodie, a bit of a weekend jetsetter and have definitely been "wined and dined" on many dates. When I was first introduced to *Tempted.com*, I was excited to see that there was a "Fine Dining" icon to "Tempt" with. I mean, I simply love to quote Samantha from *Sex and the City* when she said, "A girl's gotta eat!" I also believe that a couple who dines and plays together, stays together, so let's examine the delicious details of…**DATING AND FINE DINING.**

I cannot think of a better date than fine dining at some fancy hot spot. Since the days of black and white movies, fine dining dates have been a turn on to me! I love the idea of a man courting a woman by inviting her to dinner, the woman spending time to look and feel sexy and special, then popping open the bottle of Bordeaux or bubbly, while waiting for the filet or Caviar to arrive. Now, maybe I have watched a few too many mobster movies in my time, but when a man likes a woman, he wants to show her off and feed her well. This type of date makes me feel like chivalry is not dead! An evening of fine dining sets the tone that a man wants to spend quality time with a woman, spoiling her palate and making her feel like a princess.

Fine dining can also be incredibly sexy and sensual! The dark, dimly lit or candlelit ambiance can create an air of mystique alone. Add that bottle of *Opus One* to continue the mood and you might be on your way to a second dessert (LOL)! When experiencing a more abundant or high-end meal, people tend to savor each bite and take more time indulging in their food…and, their dates! This also allows more time for deep conversation and affection. I know I have spent many nights having my heart won over by gentleman and food at my favorites: *Mastro's Steakhouse, Bouchon, The Belvedere and The Bazaar*, to name a few.

I think *Tempted.com* fine dining "TEMPT" has so many positive purposes! If a guy is visiting Los Angeles on business and simply wants a date to a fabulous work dinner, he has an efficient method for finding that date. He may introduce her to a new world of food and fun. I think this is a wonderful situation, in which she gets a decadent dinner and, if nothing more, they each make a fantastic new friend. However, and as I mentioned earlier, I do believe that "A couple who dines and plays together, stays together" and this can lead to a long-term connection. A huge part of *Tempted.com* is "Where Temptation and Dating Connect," so if two people have fine dining in common, they have a better chance at connecting and continuing. Plus, I believe that a couple who is not shy about eating a lot together, will not be shy about doing many other things together (LOL)!

CAN A WOMAN BE INTIMATE WITH A MAN SHE IS NOT PHYSICALLY ATTRACTED TO?

It is pretty incredible how different the conversations are around physical attraction and sexual intimacy with men and women. I find it fascinating when my female clients share their dating journey's and how much their interest, affection and attraction for a man can grow, based on factors well beyond the physical. As an active online dater, I must admit that, on several occasions, I met men who I was not initially "physically" attracted to in person, yet soon became smitten with. Unlike men, I believe women can be stimulated (and, sexually turned on!) by many other qualities in a man. So, I ask you…**CAN A WOMAN BE INTIMATE WITH A MAN SHE IS NOT PHYSICALLY ATTRACTED TO?**

We all know that attraction and connection begins with phero-mones. This is the only reason I can explain and understand why I have stared at a stunning soap opera star across a dinner table on a date and felt nothing, while that other date with "average" looks made me tingle from head to toe! I do, however, believe that women are more turned on by and drawn toward certain things, than men. Women seem to love little physical things and gestures. Give me, and most of my friends, a man of "average" looks who smells great and dresses with killer style any day! We also get turned on by that guy with the straight white teeth and fresh fruity breath! And, Ladies, how sexy do we find that guy who keeps his car and house immaculately clean? Or, how much do we want to hug and cuddle with the guy who loves his Pit bull *Thor* like his child? Oh, and, the guy who just helped the lil old lady with her bags at the market? You know you want to tear him up in the parking lot (LOL)!

Speaking of "gestures", women can be swept away with romance and gifts! This is one of the reasons we are on *Tempted.com*, right, Girls? I talk about being an old-fashioned girl in some ways, but a man who romances and courts me, will find his way much faster to my heart and bedroom (LOL)! A man who wines and dines me, goes out of his way to make me feel special and "works" a bit for my affections, is a total turn-on! Looks really can only go so far with me. I have dated guys with Hollywood good looks who turned out to be the most selfish men in life and bed, while a few guys, who I was not initially attracted to, turned out to be the most giving and loving in and out of the bedroom! Guys, you know you are enticed to romance some lucky lady with a shopping spree right now (LOL)!

I believe that when women mature and enter their 30s, other qualities become more important than physical attraction. Women want, need and seek security, safety and stability (not just financial). I have been very drawn toward men who were not super physically attractive, but showed me lots of love, loyalty, support and adoration. A guy who respects and supports my career, gets a 10 on my sexy scale! When a woman feels emotionally fulfilled by a man, the attraction goes very deep and creates an even deeper need for intimacy. The same goes for mental and intellectual stimulation. My female clients consistently share how they were not "hot" for a guy at first sight, but after hours of intense and inspiring conversation, they counted down for a deep goodnight kiss! We also see a lot of women turned on by men with money. I think some women who choose men with financial success get a bad rap, but there is something truly safe and sexy about being "taken care of". Honestly, I feel more secure, while dating a man who is financially secure. I am not saying he has to be "rich", but I am much more attracted to a man who can (and, wants to!) take me fine dining and on weekend travel getaways, which eventually does lead to physical intimacy.

So, I think we have deduced that...A Woman Can Be Intimate With A Man She Is Not 'Physically' Attracted To. I understand there will be women reading this who will disagree. I also realize there are women who can, and will, only be intimate with a man she is crazily physically attracted to from the get go! I welcome and respect your individual needs and opinions.

WHY MEN SOMETIMES MOVE ON TO THE NEXT WOMAN AFTER SEX

Some may feel that, as a woman, I am not fully qualified to give my thoughts or advice on this topic, but as a Board Certified Life Coach, Dating Coach and serial dater, I would like to take a crack at it. I have female clients share, too often and with sadness and bewilderment, how they had an amazing few dates with a guy who seemed to really be into them, but, as soon as they had sex, he lost interest. I have many theories on the reasons for this, including clichés like, "Variety is the spice of life" and "Men love the conquest," but for the sake of this article, I would like to dig even deeper, so let's examine... **WHY MEN SOMETIMES MOVE ON TO THE NEXT WOMAN AFTER SEX.**

In starting with the simplest clichés mentioned above, I do believe men love variety, the conquest and to conquer (Now, listen up, Ladies!), *when* they are *not* in a place for anything serious. As men and women, we can only be ready for something "real" when we are ready. No one can control or force another person to want more or stick around after the conquest is done. When a man is fresh out of a marriage or long-term relationship, he is usually not in a place for anything exclusive. It is much easier to be physically and emotionally intimate with many people at this time, than get close and attached to just one. When a man has a relationship end, his ego is often bruised. He tends to look back and analyze all he gave to that relationship and where he failed. He needs time to get back into a power place and, sometimes, by sleeping with several women, his ego and heart start to mend. Knowing he can sexually conquer many women makes him feel like a manly man again. A similar situation can arise when a man is focused on his career. His mind and heart are married to his work at this time, and he does not have the time or energy to commit to one woman or a relationship. He is better off dating and sleeping with a variety of women, and being honest about the space he is in. I always suggest honesty, so the other person knows what she is getting into "bed" with!

I am going to address more old clichés, "Men are visual creatures" and "Men are physically stimulated". Ladies, I know you may not want to hear some of these things, but I have gathered a lot of data from clients and close male friends. Men may have had an amazing few dates with you and been super attracted to you in your sexy outfits, but when your clothes come off, the story changes. Now, let's not perceive these men as shallow and try to stay open-minded. I have heard honest feelings from men about not liking a woman's boob job, thinking a woman was too muscular, being turned off by a woman's cellulite and not finding her attractive the next morning without make-up. We cannot be mad at people for how they genuinely feel. In bringing up the physical, I have also had men tell me they stopped dating a woman after sex, because they did not like her scent, taste or the way she intimately felt. I always share that I believe there are many "someones" out there for each of us, so rather than personalizing the reasons a man moves on after sex, let's accept it and move on ourselves. In fact, let's go online and accept a date from a guy who just may love EVERYTHING about us!

Last, but not least, I believe that the world of digital dating creates a culture of "hook up" and "move on". On traditional dating sites, men seem to be taking women home for sex, after a single cocktail. Ladies, you want to take responsibility for your actions here too! Men love the chase and if we make it so easy for them to be intimate with us, they become accustomed to not having to work or court for it. I think men end up moving on to the next woman, just because they *can*! This becomes a silly game that I, and mature women, have NO interest in playing.

ONLINE DATING TIPS

AFTER 15 YEARS of online dating, I am wondering if I am no longer an Online Dating Expert, but an Online Dating Yoda (LOL)? Is there such a title these days? And, yes, you read correctly and do not need to adjust your reading glasses. I really did online date for 15 years. So, before you judge me (LOL), think about this...Who better to be an Online Dating Expert than someone who has been through it?! My goal as an Expert is to guide and support people who are online dating and help them navigate through the "horrors" of online dating, so they do not have to make the same mistakes and poor choices I made, at times. And, in full disclosure...I LOVED online dating! You can love it too and feel empowered, while playing the online dating game. Just pay attention to the coaching tips to come.

ONLINE DATING ADVICE FROM A DATING EXPERT AND DATING DRAMA QUEEN

As a single gal in Los Angeles who has been online dating for over 15 years, I have earned my stripes as a Dating Expert and a dating drama queen. I have experienced and survived all the *dramas* of online dating and still remain a *hopeful romantic*. I am here to share some coaching advice and guide and support you on your online dating journey:

IT IS IMPORTANT TO CHOOSE THE DATING SITE(S) THAT ARE RIGHT FOR WHAT/WHOM YOU ARE LOOKING FOR

Some dating sites are known and respected for finding *love* and some are notorious for attracting singles looking for *action* or a quick *hook-up*. There are no judgments here, as people are coming from different places in their love lives. If a person just got out of a 10-year marriage, he/she may not be looking for anything serious at this time. Whereas, if a person has been living single and playing the field for five years, he/she may be all-in for love. Do your homework and choose the site(s) that are right for you.

HAVE AN OBJECTIVE AND HONEST PERSON IN YOUR LIFE READ/EDIT YOUR PROFILE BEFORE YOU POST IT

You do not want to create a false perception of yourself, in either a positive or negative way. This person cannot be your Mom, because you know she will tell you that you are better than the singers on *The Voice* and that you even looked good in the pictures from college *after* you gained the freshman fifteen. Have a trusted friend or co-worker look over your profile and allow them the space to be honest.

BE HONEST IN YOUR PROFILE

If you have children, be honest about it. If you have pets, be honest about it. If you smoke, be honest about it. If you live in another state, be honest about it. If your profile is filled with lies, you are not living or sharing your truth and you will eventually be found out. I cannot tell you how many guys online have lied to me about having pets and I am *deathly* allergic. I ask the pet question in the very first email. I dated a guy for a month, really liked him and could never figure out why he didn't invite me back to his place and always wanted to stay at mine. It turned out, he had three cats. I was angry and disappointed. He went back to his cats and I went to stock up on *Zyrtec*.

Post At Least Two Photos And Make Sure One Is A Full Length Photo. Post Photos That Are Warm And Welcoming. Make Sure You Smile In One

You want to make a good first impression. Sexy photos are fine, just don't overdo it or give away too much. Trust me, this will save you time and self-esteem issues when men ask for *more full body shots*. I cannot count nor tell you how many times men have asked me for *lingerie* or *bikini* shots, but I can tell you they are not the men I am looking to date. You do not have to send *any photos* you are not comfortable with.

Make Sure The Person Contacting You Has At Least Two Photos, As Well. You Have Every Right To Ask For More

If *teeth* are important to you, ask for a smiling photo. If you are a sucker for *pretty eyes*, ask for a photo without sunglasses. I met a gorgeous guy online once. He had several photos posted, but none smiling. I am always wary, because that tells me something about someone's personality. Regardless, I took a chance and met him. I wasn't too surprised when he smiled and had discolored and missing teeth. I'm not judging, but it didn't make me want to kiss him.

You Do Not Have To Respond To Every Contact You Receive

Be as *kind* and *considerate* as possible, but you do not *owe* anyone anything. Being a sweet gal, I used to spend hours responding to emails from men by saying, "No, thank you" and kindly explaining the reasons I did not feel we were a match. Often, men could not take the rejection and would respond with some nasty remark. Your time is valuable. Don't waste it.

Make Sure You Have A Full Length Phone Conversation Before You Meet For A Date

This does not mean a full *text conversation*. Take the time to see if you *click* and have a *connection* worth pursuing in person. Trust your *intuition*. When I pay attention to my intuition and actually follow it, it rarely fails me. You want to ask questions, really listen (red flags), see how you *feel* in the conversation and make sure the person on the other end of the phone is not *certifiably insane*. We are all a little kooky, but you know what I mean.

Meet In Public And On Neutral Territory

Take your own *car* and do not go to someone's *home*. In being authentic (and, a HOT MESS!), I will share that I have made this mistake a few times and it rarely turned out well. More than once, I have asked a guy to drive me home before we ever got to the restaurant and one time, I literally threw an aggressive guy out of my home at the end of a first date. Be smart and safe and do as I say, not as I did.

Make Your First Date A Brief One

I recommend *coffee* or a *drink*. Give yourself a responsible *out*, if you need it. This is a strong rule I commit to. I made a lot of mistakes online dating when I started and definitely learned the hard way. If you plan an extravagant evening with someone you have never met, you will regret it if he/she looks nothing like his/her photos, you have zero chemistry and the conversation is empty.

No Sex On The First Date

Okay, you're an adult and if you want it, *choose* it...*but*, know that when things happen too quickly, they often fizzle fast too. Just remember that you are the only one who has to sleep on your pillow at night and wake up with yourself and your choices in the morning.

TOP 5 PET PEEVES OF ONLINE DATING

As a Dating Coach and Expert, as well as a single woman who has online dated far too long (LOL!), I have heard about and experienced these obvious online dating "pet peeves" more than I can count, but whether new to online dating or needing confirmation for your online dating sanity (LOL!), let's cover some frequent issues:

LYING & MISREPRESENTING

Statistically, women are notorious for lying about their age and weight and men their height and income, and I am not even mad about it anymore (LOL)! The deeper lies are what get my clients and me. If you have children, say so. If you have pets, say so. If you smoke, say so. If you live in another state, say so. Tell the truth and allow the person to choose if they want to be with you. You are YOU and you have nothing to hide. Lying and misrepresenting is no way to create a healthy and real relationship and you will eventually be found out!

NOT POSTING AT LEAST 3 PHOTOS & 1 FULL LENGTH

This peeve should be in the online dating handbook (LOL)! I learned years ago never to respond to a profile that contains only one photo or headshot. We have all experienced a situation in which we fall instantly "in love" (or, lust!) with a person's main profile picture, only to move to photo #2 and learn that the Brad Pitt look-alike has suddenly transformed into *Quasimodo*! And, male clients and friends constantly complain to me about how their date had gorgeous head-shots on her profile, then seemed to gain 100 lbs. between the time they ended their call and met in person! Now, I am not telling you to be shallow or all about the physical by any means, but posting photo options will save each of you some disappointment (notice I said "some" LOL!).

ENDLESS EMAILS & PHONE CALLS

I will bet my bottom dollar that if you continue endless email correspondence and even constant phone calls without meeting pretty early on, you will end up wasting time and not meeting at all! As an Expert, I recommend having a few substantial phone conversations (NOT TEXT!), then planning a date within two weeks! Life happens and we are all super busy these days, but we can make time to meet for an hour drink or latte! Remember, with online dating, there is a new profile being "swiped" every minute (LOL)!

LONG-DISTANCE DATING

At first long-distance dating seems fun, exciting, romantic and every visit is like a holiday! But, unless one partner in the relationship is willing to move to the other partner's state, it will never work long-term! I have experienced this firsthand several times, until I learned my lesson and I have clients who jump on the long-distance train, only to return with baggage and tears in hand! Remember, you have no idea what goes on when you are not there! And, worse, it has become an online dating trend now for men to so "graciously" fly a woman out for a romantic weekend, simply to have a fresh new face to share one weekend of wild sex with! Ladies, if you are down, more power to you! I just want you to choose powerfully!

DATE INVITATION TO "COME TO MY HOME"

Okay, so I am going to be a total hypocrite here, but an honest one (LOL)! I have done it and it does not usually end well. Either the guy looked nothing like his photo and I wanted him out in five minutes or we had instant sexual chemistry and that leads to trouble! Ladies, do NOT ever go to a strange guy's home! And, men, let's get back to basics and start asking women out on proper dates again! I hear this complaint all the time from both men and women. They tell me how they met someone online or on *Tinder* and it was late and they were tired and just wanted to "hangout", so they went to a stranger's home and drank a few bottles of wine. Of course, pretty soon other things were "hangin' out" (LOL)! Just realize that when you put yourself in an intimate setting without others around and add cocktails to the mix, it creates an illusion of real intimacy that does not exist on a first date! Chances are that if you start your relationship as a "booty call", you will end your relationship as a "booty call"!

TOP 3 REASONS PEOPLE LIE IN THEIR ONLINE DATING PROFILES

After online dating for over 15 years, then creating a profession out of it, I do not think there is a single lie I have not seen, heard or experienced. We all know the standard online dating lies at this point, where women are notorious for lying about their age and weight and men about their height and income, but I am addressing bigger lies and the professional (and, personal!) reasons I believe people often lie in their dating profiles. Three will not do this justice, but let's start here:

PEOPLE GENUINELY BELIEVE THEY ARE WHO THEY PORTRAY

I have debated this subject with many people, many times. Male clients have expressed with frustration, "There's no way she really thinks she is "athletic and toned"!" Unfortunately, this is one of the subjective things we cannot make sense of in life. What one person thinks "thin" looks like, another may not and what one person thinks "smart" means, another may not. I try to give people online the benefit of the doubt and realize that they genuinely believe they are who they portrayed themselves to be. Maybe a woman had a mother tell her how gorgeous she was since birth and she grew up fully believing it. It is actually a wonderful thing and we should all be so lucky to feel good about ourselves.

PEOPLE THINK THEY CAN MAKE YOU BELIEVE THEY ARE WHO THEY PORTRAY

This one is a bit trickier and can be done unconsciously or manipulatively! These people are aware that they are lying or manipulating information or your perception of them, yet they continue to do so, without a harmful intention. I truly believe they do not mean to be hurtful by misleading you, but they desperately want to make you like or fall for them. They believe that by giving you the information you want to hear, you will eventually like them and want to meet them. They believe that if they post false photos, physical statistics, income level or a closer location, you will eventually fall for them and none of this will matter. You know…the person who has the perfect profile and personality on the phone, but is 10 years older and looks like a different person when you actually meet?! Like the old cliché states, "If it seems too good to be true, it probably is!"

PEOPLE HAVE A HIDDEN AGENDA OR SECRET

In my opinion, this is the worst lie of all! Even if the person's agenda or intention is not of ill-will or harmful in any way, that person is entering into a dating situation or relationship without truth or honesty. I understand that there are things that should not be revealed to the world and that we all have secrets! I would never advise someone to disclose information that could damage another person, however, I do advise to share the truth privately and allow the person on the other end to responsibly choose! I am deathly allergic to animals and have so many dating stories of guys who listed "No Pets" in their profiles, started relationships with me, then a month in, when I asked to come to their homes, revealed their roommate named *Spike*! I also have 100 stories about men who lied about having children, living in another state or the profession they were in. I am a smart cookie, so I was quick to discover these lies, but notice, I am NOT with these men! I believe people keep these secrets and lies, because they do not want to face whatever it is they are dealing with. I often think these people are running away from their problems and toward on-line dating, because they CAN get away with hiding the truth! I think that somewhere in their minds, they believe they are starting with a "clean slate". I have clients complain that they met someone they liked who listed "divorced", then turned out to be newly "separated". I say, offer the info and let the person choose.

REASONS TO START WITH A COFFEE OR DRINKS DATE

As a serial online dater, Coach and Expert, I have made many mistakes and learned a lot of lessons. One of the simplest and most valuable lessons I have learned is NOT to commit too much time to someone on a first date or meeting. I KNOW those of you who have online dated will agree! I recommend easing into a first encounter for many reasons. From physical attraction, mental attraction, safety, honesty, agreements and arrangements, there are components of a first interaction that are pertinent to a connection and where it will go casually or seriously. A great thing about *Tempted.com* is it has options that allow you to start with a casual coffee or drinks date, before jumping into a week of travel with someone who is not who he/she pretends to be (or, someone who posted photos from 10 years ago!). At *Tempted.com*, you can play a fun dating game and work your way up to those hot, steamy nights on a tropical island! So, let's learn the...**REASONS TO START WITH A COFFEE OR DRINKS DATE**.

Online daters often confuse what IS real with what they WANT to be real. I have been guilty of seeing photos and reading a profile and thinking a guy was my soul mate or *Prince Charming*, then feeling completely deflated when we met in person. When I started online dating many years ago, I got caught up in the excitement of the romance and mystery and would accept long, planned out dates, only to be disappointed most of the time. It takes time to get to know someone and you want to put yourself in a situation that allows you to have a real conversation in a real public place to learn about this real person, as best you can. You want to give yourself an out, if things are not going well. There is nothing worse than feeling trapped on a date that you cannot leave. I do not care how good looking someone is, because if he/she is rude or crazy, I'm leaving! I mean, we know this is more than likely to happen here in Los Angeles (LOL)! So, I say we start with a coffee or drinks date, then choose our next move (or, not!).

Another reason to start with coffee or drinks, then work your dates up is to allow or create the tone for something to build or grow. Whether you are seeking an ongoing relationship, a companion for a season of *Lakers* games or someone to accompany you on business trips, you want to give it room to grow and allow the experiences to build. I talk about how when things happen too fast, they tend to fizzle fast too. I think spending a chill and romantic night, sipping drinks on the beach in Malibu, while getting to know one another is a perfect set-up for dates of travel to come. By spending a quality date with someone, you can get to know more than you think.

ONLINE DATING AND AGEISM

Have I ever lied about my age? If I tell you I have not, I would be lying twice. I recently met a guy online who I quickly discovered was 10 years older than his profile stated. I was so frustrated, thought about how this had happened to me more times than I can count throughout my online dating history and felt compelled to share some of my theories about *online dating and ageism* and how to handle it.

Changing Your Age Puts You Into A Different Search

After meeting many men online who have lowered their age by 10 to 12 years, I had to learn what this was about (other than *deception*). Some men have been forthright enough to reveal their real age on the first phone call, others have done so on the first date and I have *shockingly* discovered the rest on my own at our first face-to-face, when I am expecting a 38-year-old and in walks a 50-year-old in his place (and, let me tell you that I *love* dating older men, it is the *surprise* that is my issue). I have to admit that the explanations have been fair and consistent. Both men I have met and my female clients have shared that they ended up in a much smaller search group when they listed their true age. Many men and women feel that they have the energy and stamina at 50 to date a 35-year-old. And, why not? More power to them. I have also experienced the opposite on certain online dating sites where you can regulate the age of people who contact you. Ladies, there are quite a few 22-year-old guys who seem to love a sexy older woman, so they list their age as older, then give their true age in the body of their profile and explain how they are much more attracted to older women. Hmmm…maybe we can accept this explanation.

Many Men Search For Women Who Are Within Childbearing Age

This is a theory that I completely understand, but in some ways has always fascinated me. Statistics show that the age range for child-bearing women is primarily 20-35. I have found that more and more men and women are focused on and building their careers and businesses through their 40s and even 50s. Biologically, this can create a challenge for women, if they want to bear their own children. Men, on the other hand, can pull a *Tony Randall* and reproduce at 75. I authentically believe that we should all go after and create everything we want in life, so I encourage men to court younger women, if they dream of having biological children. The part that always fascinates me is when I receive emails from men who are in their 60s (my Dad's age) and I think about what we might have in common and how he will be 80 when our child is in college.

PEOPLE GENUINELY HAVE A SKEWED VIEW OF WHO THEY ARE AND WHOM THEY SHOULD DATE

Yes, it is normal to date 20 years younger and much hotter in Hollywood, but I would like to address the rest of the world here. I have shared this in many online dating articles and I stand firmly on the fact that many people truly do have a false perception of themselves. Remember, people can create anything they want to in an online dating profile and post 10-year-old photos, as well. It makes me sad to think that people still want to hold on to whom they were and what they looked like 20 years ago, rather than embracing who they are now…wrinkles, extra few pounds and all. Rather than a *mature* gentleman emailing a much younger *Trophy wife*, I suggest he contact women around his age or a few years younger, as he may discover that there are many women over 40 who are equally as beautiful, fit, active, fun, sexy and sensual as the 25-year-old *chippy* in the previous profile. And, those *mature* women may appreciate this man way more.

PEOPLE DO NOT WANT THEIR PERSONAL INFORMATION ONLINE

This justification may not really involve ageism, but I actually understand and respect the rationale behind it, and feel it is important for you to think about. I had a high profile, successful client who explained that he changed his birthdate by a year and a half, because he did not want strangers knowing his personal information to research him and his businesses online. I realize that *privacy* is *not* part of the internet and when you put yourself out there, you risk everyone finding out who you are, where you live and where you ate dinner last night, but I also know it is important to protect your privacy when you are in the public eye.

SEXTING AND NAKED PHOTOS WITH ONLINE DATING

As an Online Dating Expert, I have been asked about this topic several times on TV and radio, and as a single woman online dating for years, I have personally experienced this stomach-churning situation more times than I ever cared to, so I think it is important to address...**SEXTING AND NAKED PHOTOS WITH ONLINE DATING**.

Listen guys, I, and most women, are all in favor of a little sexy, flirty *iPhone* fun, but I have been trying to figure out when the boundaries got crossed (And, ladies, you are not innocent here either!). As a Coach, you will hear me speak about how inappropriate it is to get to know someone via text, in the first place, but this sexting and sending "t*t" and "d*ck" pics has become ridiculous and disrespectful! I am all in favor of online urgency and instant gratification, but rather than sharing a picture of your "package" after a 10-minute text conversation, how about saving that surprise for the romantic weekend of travel in person (LOL)?

Whenever I have had sessions and conversations with my female clients and friends about this, we have deduced that some woman, somewhere, confirmed with men that this digital behavior was acceptable, and now we are paying the price (Again, ladies, you are not innocent here either! LOL!). So, ladies, next time you get the urge to send a naked photo or super sexual sentence to a guy you have never even spoken with yet, I want you to ask yourself the reason you are doing it. I fear, sometimes, that digital dating has made dating so competitive for women, they will do anything out of desperation. I also fear that in this day of the social media craze, women will do anything they can to receive attention, especially that of a man. I have news for you, ladies, I know a lot of classy, successful men who have no interest in seeing your naked booty on their smartphones (unless, of course, it looks like *JLO's*!).

Now, guys, I understand you are...MEN! I understand that most of you think about sex (and, food!) like all day, every day (LOL)! That said (and, please trust the word of this woman who has dated a lot!), most of the classy men I have met on dating sites and successfully dated, did NOT (and, would NOT!) "sext" me, nor send "d*ck" pics! Ironically, the few that did, I chose not to go out with or, after a few dates, they proved to be disrespectful in some other way. I understand that by nature, men like to push the envelope (and, boundaries!) and they want to see what a woman is willing to give them. It is human nature for a man to want sex or something sexual from a woman and there is nothing wrong with this. The problem arises when the woman accepts the man's advances, they become intimate quickly (this includes sexting and naked pics!), then the man loses interest or no longer wants to see the woman and she loses her mind…and, self-esteem along with it! I believe that unless both parties have a mutual agreement and respect for one another, nothing good can come of this.

This topic moves me right toward all the reasons I love *Tempted. com*! This dating site offers so many sexy and fun dating connections and experiences. These options are enticing enough, so you might not need to send naked pics. If you feel the need for frisky photos, however, you do have the private photo section for those lucky enough to get a sneak peek. Listen, we pass no judgment at *Tempted.com* and you are free to "sext" all you want, but something tells me that you will be much more motivated to play in our grown-ups Playground where mutual respect and temptation is endless and you can expose yourself where, when and how you choose. I mean, I would much prefer to show my goods, while skinny-dipping in Greece, wouldn't you?

TOP 5 REASONS MEN WANT TO TEMPT A WOMAN

While pitching article ideas to my bosses, as the *Tempted.com Dating Expert & Spokesperson*, I was fairly certain I would send this topic over to one of our male blog contributors. However, the more I got to thinking about this, the more inspired I became to delve into the male psyche for a moment and express my thoughts on the…**TOP 5 REASONS MEN WANT TO TEMPT A WOMAN.**

To Pursue and Court A Woman

As liberated as women (including myself!) and dating, in general, have become, I still believe that men innately want, and need, to pursue and court a woman! Men want to work for and earn a woman's attention and affection. *Tempted.com* offers a quick and efficient way for a man to reach out and "Tempt" a woman, and he has several options to choose from. They have the option to keep it simple with a quick cocktail or court bigtime with a weekend away!

The Challenge

Listen, Ladies! If there is one thing I have discovered for sure, it is that men love a challenge! From childhood to adulthood, boys will be boys and, whether in sports, business or dating, they will be hard-pressed to back down from something they want. The gorgeous thing about *Tempted.com* is that women can let men know what they are seeking from the start! If a woman loves fancy-pants gifts, shopping and fine dining, she is empowered to say so. That said, I love this part of the Tempted game, where a man might "Tempt" a woman with coffee, she might not "Accept" his "Tempt" and he will "Tempt" her again with the fine dining icon, so he can receive a "yes". Now, that seems like a fun challenge!

COMPETITION WITH OTHER MEN

Similar to the reason above, but deserving its own mention, men thrive on competition with other men. As a single woman, who has dated a lot of successful men, I learned early on that men will do just about anything to compete for that promotion at work, the larger office, the faster car or the gorgeous girlfriend. And, as a Life Coach, I stand behind the idea that there is nothing wrong with a "healthy" ego or competition. At *Tempted.com*, men know that women will be receiving some very enticing "Tempt" dates, so they may want to step up their game and compete for that lovely Lady who caught their eye. Wait, did I just read front row *Lakers* seats? Game on!

TO SHARE WHAT THEY HAVE WORKED HARD FOR

Successful men tend to be very proud of their accomplishments. They also tend to want to share what they have worked hard for with the people they care about. At *Tempted.com*, you will find a lot of successful and/or abundant men who have worked toward accomplishing their career goals most of their adult lives, and are now in a place to share it with another person. As I have stated before, some of my favorite men to date are the ones who have been divorced, started over and want to share their lives, things and time with someone new and special. This time around, they want to feel appreciated for what they share with us!

TO MAKE HER FEEL SPECIAL

I saved this for last, because it is surely not least! I know there are a lot of jaded ladies out there in online dating land. I also know you have every right to feel hurt and frustrated, after putting yourselves out there and having some lousy experiences! That said, and acknowledged, I promise you that most men do want to make a woman feel special! I have heard time and time again from male clients and friends that they are most happy when they make the woman they are with happy! When a man truly likes, cares for or loves a woman, he will go to great lengths to make her feel special. *Tempted.com* offers men a fun way to date and treat a woman like a Queen.

REAL MEN STILL WANT TO PAMPER WOMEN

As a woman who has dated and coached many men, I have learned lessons about men that are vast and indispensable. As human beings, I truly believe we want to love and be loved, beyond anything else. I also believe that men and women tend to express themselves and their love in different ways. I have learned that men can behave and show their love in very different forms than other men. I have experienced men who share and show their feelings through affection and compliments, others through gifts, others through financial support, others through random acts of kindness, and others through all of the above. I have also grown to understand that there will be times when a man is not in a place to give love or anything strong, heavy or intense, due to his present circumstances or situation (A great time to join *Tempted.com*!), but, no matter what, I have learned that...**REAL MEN STILL WANT TO PAMPER WOMEN.**

I realize sometimes I sound a bit old school in my thinking, but I still believe in the theory that the man should chase, initiate, court and pursue. I believe this goes beyond ego and that psychologically and physiologically, a man wants to "win" a woman, whether it be temporarily or long-term. This is one of the reasons men want to pamper women. A man instinctually knows that if he makes a woman feel safe, secure, adored or loved, she will open her heart, body, mind and soul to him. Other than career and financial success, I feel this is one of man's greatest conquests (And, yes, it can be for a lifetime or "one-weekend-stand"!). Whether a man is trying to take a woman to bed or to the alter, he is still working to "win" her in some way and knows that fine dining, the expensive bottle of champagne, taking her shopping for that *Louis Vuitton* bag or paying for her precious *Fluffy's* vet bill, will make her feel special, taken care of or cared for.

I mentioned earlier and think it is important to address that men are not always in a place to enter a relationship or anything serious, yet I still believe they want to pamper women in a different way. This is when I love to brag how *Tempted.com* has something for everyone! As we get older and more men are going through divorces and in the thick of their careers, their agendas may be to pamper differently. A man who is newly separated or running a Fortune 500 company may not have the time or emotions to give to a woman. Ladies, sometimes these are the men who will pamper you the most! I have discovered that these men know that they are not capable of the emotional pampering at this time, so they are more generous with their gifts and material spoiling to let you know they care. They may not be able to fully open their hearts and calendars at this time, but they will pamper you and make you feel special in whatever way they can. Hmmm…this is making me hopeful that one of these guys will "Tempt" me with my fave dinner at *Mastro's Steakhouse* soon…just because he knows I love the petite filet with lobster mashed potatoes and wants to see me smile. That is my kinda pampering!

DEAR BROOKE

OF COURSE, I was inspired by *DEAR ABBY,* as a young girl! I mean, what woman wasn't? As I became more known in the public, as a Life and Dating Coach, I began to receive more and more advice questions via email and social media. I have had a few different advice columns over the years from *Huffington Post* to *SheKnows* to *Tempted.com,* so I thought I would pick some of my favorite Q&A posts and share them with you. It is fascinating to see how much we can learn from other people's issues, so you might find answers to your very own questions or dating dilemmas in this chapter.

DEAR BROOKE

DATING YOUNGER MEN

ALANA: What do you think about women dating younger men? My boyfriend is fifteen years younger than I am. Is this crazy or could it really be true love?

BROOKE: Alana, I am so glad you emailed me this question, because there are so many women wanting an answer to this right now! Although it has been happening for ages (especially in European countries), the Demi Moore/Ashton Kutcher and Cameron Diaz/Justin Timberlake unions seemed to set a trend a few years back, making the "older woman/ younger man" relationship hip and sexy. It became more "acceptable" in our society, seemed to empower women and surely gave women more options to choose from. Plus, any time something happens in Hollywood, it must be real, right? Now, let's look at where both couples mentioned above are today and discuss what IS real.

As a Life and Dating Coach, I do not judge and I will give you my professional objective opinion. Before I go there, however, I do want to share my experience with you. As a single woman, I have had many relationships with all different types of men. One of the true "loves of my life", and the only man I have ever lived with, was a younger man. He was one of the most gorgeous, sexy, passionate, doting, loving, supportive men I have ever dated. He pursued me like crazy and I fell hard…hard enough to ignore everything that my intuition was telling me…hard enough to let him move in with me. I was very clear to share my future wants and needs with him upfront, including the fact that I wanted to continue to live in Los Angeles, that I did not want to have children and that I was very focused on my career. He agreed that he was on the same page with everything… and, I dove right in! How I could have thought that a guy in his mid-twenties could possibly know exactly what he wanted for his future,

I will never understand. I do, however, understand that sometimes love makes us blind to the real truth. After our Honeymoon stage of living together, things began to get more clear. I discovered that my guy was still drinking and partying like a fraternity brother, was in the process of changing careers and wasn't sure what he wanted to do, was greatly missing his life and family on the east coast and was still truly experimenting in life. I remember watching *"The Break-Up"* with Jennifer Aniston and Vince Vaughn one night and thinking, "Oh no! This is my life!" After a year of living together, things went south and we started to resent each other. I felt like he was my son and he felt like I was behaving like his mother (I mentioned earlier that I did not want children, right?) and when a relationship turns into that dynamic, there is nothing *sexy* about it! We had a bad break-up and I was left heart-broken and beating myself up over knowing it would end like this, but choosing it anyway! The happy ending is that a year after the break-up, he reached out to me and we had a power-ful and loving conversation and we are friends to this day, and I can honestly say I learned a great deal from that relationship. I can also honestly say that I have dated men who were much older than I, yet still behaved more immaturely and irresponsibly than my younger man (LOL)!

So, as a Life and Dating Coach, what do I think about women dating younger men and is this crazy or could it really be true love? Well, if we were in a coaching session, I would first ask what YOU think? I feel like since you emailed this question, you are either hav-ing some doubts yourself or you are listening to the chatter of others whom are making your choice wrong. Could it really be true love? You betcha! I support the idea that true love does not discriminate… it comes in all shapes, sizes, colors, ages, genders and can be the most incredible feeling in the world! We all know the old saying, "You can't choose who you fall in love with!" Well, I coach around the idea that true POWER lies in our CHOICES in every moment! That said, I believe that we can fall in love with someone and still CHOOSE to be or not to be in a relationship with him. So, let's talk about whether you are choosing powerfully and responsibly. You will hear me talk about "taking responsibility" for our actions, choices and lives quite often. You will also hear me say, "With every choice, there is a consequence." What are the consequences (not good, nor bad…simply results!) you face by dating a man fifteen years younger? Now, we know you never ask a lady her age, so I am going to pretend that you are forty-five and your boyfriend is thirty (and, again, I recently went on a date with a fifty year old guy (much older than I!) who was divorced and lived in a house with two other guys, so bear with me for the sake of helping Alana here!). Is he able to share in or meet your financial needs or are you picking up most of the checks? Does he want to have his own children one day and what happens if he chooses to do so in ten years from now? Do you enjoy the same places and activities or are you uncomfortable hanging out with him at bars where everyone is under 30? How do you *feel about yourself* when you are with him…does he make you feel younger or do you feel too old for him. How does it make you feel when people stare and notice the age difference? And, sadly, but in keeping it real, what happens in fifteen years when he is forty-five and you are sixty? I know today women are looking hotter and better than ever as they age, but will true love endure and will this younger man look past the natural physical changes that occur at sixty? I cannot predict the future and neither can you, but only you are in your relationship and only you can know what your heart and gut tells you! I believe we need to live in the now, the moment, and not guess so much about what the future holds, but I do believe in taking responsibility for our choices, so that IF our relationships end, we understand and are clear that we allowed ourselves to be in that experience and the heartbreak is ours to OWN!

DEAR BROOKE

MARRIED MAN, BUT MY BEST FRIEND IS A WOMAN

TREVOR: My best friend is a woman. My wife, for the most part, is fine with this. There have never been any feelings beyond friendship. However, recently, I've found myself seething with jealousy over the guys my friend dates. Part of me feels that they're not good enough for her. Part of me doesn't want her to find someone in her life, because I know that when she does, no matter how selfish this may sound, I'll be replaced -- at least on an emotional level. Of course, I want her to be happy and to find someone special. How can I juggle the feelings of insecurity and remain her friend, even if she makes choices that I don't agree with?

BROOKE: Trevor, first and foremost, I really want to acknowledge you for your self-awareness and being in touch with your emotions and feelings. I think a lot of married men and women have emotionally intimate relationships with members of the opposite sex (or same sex, if you are in a gay marriage!) and are not able to admit to their feelings of jealousy and insecurity. The second most important thing I want to touch upon in this Q&A conversation is absolute RESPECT for your WIFE! I can feel my married readers (especially the women!) getting angry through the computer screen, as they read your question. I am pleased that you stated in your question, "There have never been any feelings beyond friendship." Now, if I were in a full coaching session with you, I would ask a number of questions around that statement to make sure that it is genuinely true and accurate. So, for the sake of this advice column, I am going to accept what you state as truth and we are going to be certain that your wife has nothing to be concerned about and you are always putting your vow and commitment to her first with any of your outside friendships. We can now move on to what this is really about and that is YOU and your feelings that you have been generous and open enough to share with the world. No judgments here!

Now, Trevor, I don't think that you are "in love" with your best female friend, but I am hearing some serious anxiety, fears and control issues going on for you underneath this...and, it is totally "normal"! When we care deeply for another person, whether it be a family member, friend or co-worker (with whom we spend many hours throughout the day and why the terms "work husband" and "work wife" were invented!), it is normal to develop an emotionally intimate attachment to her/him and fear that it could be taken away! Now, I want to remove the opposite sex part for a moment and look at life and relationships in general. Life happens, things change and we move forward every day! We all know that some things we can control by the choices we make, but controlling others and their choices is not one of them...and why would we want to? The reason is our own FEAR...fear of loss, fear of not being loved, fear of being "less than", fear of change and many others. I had a best girlfriend who I was inseparable with from 17-25. We went clubbing together, shopping together, double-dated together, traveled together, laughed and cried together and did stupid things that young people do together! Then, she met him! Out of all the guys she dated, I never would have imagined she'd choose him to marry! He was so different than us in every way (including, not having our fun and carefree personalities), but she married him and now has four kids with him. I mean, she and I were like two-peas-in-a-pod...how could she choose him and more importantly, why was I so upset? I was upset because I was losing the past..."the way we were"! I feared the change in our dynamic and I felt an emptiness and aloneness deep inside. Well, things did change, but I accepted her choices and loved her still the same. We were never as close once they married, but I will cherish that friendship forever, because it was such a part of my life and growth. I have another life experience to share about one of my best guy friends, since right out of college, in NYC. I had just graduated from college and had moved into an actors' hotel residence in NYC. One day, I saw this cute guy walking into his room right next door to mine. I was instantly drawn to this guy and our lifelong friendship began! We were soon joined at the hip! We did everything together (not sexually!). As they say on one of my fave shows, *Grey's Anatomy*, he was my "person"! We were young and single and running around NYC, living our dream as actors. We shared the same taste in food, music, movies, clothes and were as close as a brother and sister could be! We went to dinner with each other's families when they came to town and we were each other's "plus 1" to every event. He soon moved to Los Angeles to further pursue his career and I followed a year later. We started all over again and partied like Rock Stars with our new LA posse. Then, it happened! Before he had left NYC, he had met a beautiful Broadway dancer who was crazy about him and had been thinking of making the move, as well. They stayed in touch and she eventually came out for a "visit", which turned into a permanent visit. Talk about being "replaced", Trevor! She quickly joined our posse and I felt confused, insecure and surely, at first, wasn't sure if she was "good enough" for him either (sounding familiar?). Then, one night I took a step back and really observed the two of them together…they were happy, she adored him, he seemed to be really smitten with her, they worked and most importantly behaved like they were "best friends". So, I thought, "Well, if they are best friends and he is my best friend, maybe she could become one of my best friends too?" and the rest was history! I really gave her a chance and took the time to get to know her. She was not only beautiful, but talented, smart, classy, sweet and a good person. She loved my friend so much, he was happy… and how could that not make me happy? Isn't that what we want for the people we love…for them to find someone to love them and make them happy (I bet your best girlfriend is happy that you have a wife who loves you so much)? That said, the story ends with me having been in their wedding party a few years back and I am still close with both of them!

Something I speak and coach about often is the theory that you cannot have love and fear in the same space! If you truly love your best friend, CHOOSE not to fear losing her or her friendship to another guy she might fall for. I get that this is not easy, but choose it anyway! Another thing I want to point out is that underneath all the yucky feelings of jealousy and insecurity that you mentioned, lies a lack of TRUST…trust in yourself and trust in your friendship! We tend to lose trust in ourselves, others, *God* and the *Universe* when we fear a loss of someone/something. So, rather than go to the negative emotions, I want you to get into a positive feeling space. Next time you feel this way, think about a wonderful, happy time/experience that you and your best friend had together. Remember and relay the details. Our positive thoughts create our positive feelings, so allow yourself to feel all that is precious and cherished in your friendship. I bet you will be feeling better about this in no time. And, I bet if you allow yourself to open up to the idea that your friendship is forever and true and no one can "replace" what you have (he can only add to it!), you might just end up with a really cool new best guy friend and have a blast double-dating with them and your wife one day!

DEAR BROOKE

Guys Online Are Consumed With A Woman's Body

AMANDA: Drama Queen, I am a single woman in San Diego who joined online dating last year. I think I am in decent shape, but I'm not a skinny girl. I work out and eat fairly healthy, but I'm not fanatical about it. I feel like the guys online are consumed with a woman's body and are looking for "perfection". I am constantly being asked for more photos and full length body shots. When did men become so shallow and why is it making me feel so bad about myself and my body? Any advice, because I am "Insecure In San Diego"?

BROOKE: Amanda, welcome to the "Single Girls Insecure Club"! I chose your question out of all the submissions this week, because I am the President of this club (LOL!)! Seriously though, I chose your question, because it struck a chord, as I have been through this too many times and can sooo relate! I also know that many of my female readers (And, single male readers!) can relate too! In fact, this just happened to me a few times recently with online dating, so I am freshly prepared to vent with you!

As a Life and Dating Coach, I will get to my objective professional advice later, but, first I want to share my personal experiences with you, as a fellow single chick. Like you, Amanda, I fancy myself a fairly "attractive" woman. I am an actress, as well, and have received fan mail with ridiculously flattering compliments, so I must not be too scary (Jokes the Scream Queen)! That said, I am very aware of my strengths and weaknesses! I am a very conscientious person who works out and commits to healthy eating about five days a week. I do, however, feel that there is a healthy "balance" to life and I refuse to starve myself or base everything on the physical, like my actress friends and I did when we were young! By nature, I am short, curvy and voluptuous! I will never be a tall, skinny Hollywood actress, nor

Supermodel, and I am really okay with it! I have no shortage of men telling me how much they like my plump booty (Please bear with me and my self-praise for the sake of this column)! My point here is that, like you, I should NOT have to make excuses nor apologies for myself or my body, yet, I find myself doing so all the time with the men in Los Angeles! Now, I want to be fair to the men for a moment and acknowledge that my issues and insecurities are mine to OWN! However, I have experienced your complaint with men and online dating more than I cared to and I feel it needs to be addressed. I mean, I am still a little old school and I believe in respect and the rule that a true gentleman never asks a lady her age or weight. I think I am very fair and reasonable with the photos I post on the online dating sites, I make certain I always have a few full body shots posted and I list my body type as "average". That should be enough to give a guy a pretty clear idea of whom he is going to meet, right? So, I wonder why so many men find it necessary to ask for more photos or photos of me in bikinis or lingerie!? I, too, find this so disrespectful and I start to feel like there is something *wrong* with me! This brings up all my body image issues and I feel myself going right to the space of *not feeling good enough*! Then, I have to check and coach myself and ask, "Wait, I don't feel good enough for WHOM?" Really? I allow myself to not feel good enough for the *disrespectful guy I don't want to date in the first place* (Ya feel me, Amanda?)?

This situation is hilarious and just happened to me a few weeks ago. I received an email from a guy online. He looked handsome in his photos and posted that he was 45, although I kept thinking he looked at least ten years older than that. I gave him my number after a few emails and he texted me, asking for more full body shots. I told him he had already seen a few and wanted to know why he needed more. He texted me that, "He is a very handsome, successful man and ONLY dates beautiful, in-shape younger women." Of course, at this point I was ready to "throw up in my mouth", but I entertained him! He then proceeded to tell me that he ONLY dates women who wear clothing between the sizes of 0-6. He guessed that on a "good" day, I wear a 2 and on a "bad" day, I wear a 4 (This is when my mouth opened and I grabbed the barf bag!). Funny thing is, he actually nailed my true sizes, but I thought to myself, "How could I ever date this shallow idiot?" and then I thought, "Either he worked in women's retail or he's *Buffalo Bill* from *Silence Of The Lambs'* little brother!" Either one, I was done! But, I just had to ask his REAL age, before I excused myself from the call and sure enough, he admitted he was 56! I only add this, because at 56, you would think he would know better and be more evolved, and now we know he is not only shallow, but a liar! Then, I had another guy pursue me online for quite some time and when I finally agreed to talk to him, he asked if I would email him photos of my butt and thighs first, as he could not date women with cellulite and required photos of this before meeting any of his dates in person. This one went beyond my shallow meter and raised my fetish or freak red flag!

Okay, now that I am done with my "frustrated single woman venting" bit, I will go Life and Dating Coach on our butts! There is so much great stuff in your question to dissect that I will only scratch the surface on each issue. First, I want to point out the issue of the INTERNET! I always feel it is a blessing and a curse! The internet has given people the opportunity, forum and COURAGE to hide behind a screen and say things or behave in a way they NEVER would in person! Sometimes it can be a scary place and I believe this carries over to online dating! In some ways, I feel that online dating dismisses the "courting process", which I happen to be a big fan of! I feel as though men are no longer required to act like gentleman and, in their defense, women often forget to act like ladies! I think that online dating sites are so fully loaded with "options" that both men and women feel they have the right to be disrespectful and make demands. People have the attitude like, "There's another bus coming around the corner" and in many ways, this is true! It becomes a quantity over quality thing and when so many women are posting profiles in bikinis and lingerie, men think they have the right to ask the rest of us for photos like that, as well. I understand some of my female readers will take offense to this, but, in keeping it real, I do feel that in some ways, women are to blame for men's poor and disrespectful behavior! The more we give them what they want, the more they think it is acceptable and ap-propriate to ask or expect. Let's remember, ladies, that men are visual creatures! They want to see as much as they can before buying the goods! So, when a guy has just looked at twenty photos of women in their bra and panties or the last six women he exchanged numbers with texted him half-naked photos, he thinks he has the right to ask us for them, as well! Make a little more sense now?

More importantly, Amanda, it is the way we handle this and take responsibility for it that matters! We make CHOICES and can choose not to give away our POWER or allow men to make us feel a certain way about ourselves and our bodies! I always find it spiritually and metaphysically fascinating that when I am feeling insecure about my body or weight, I tend to attract men who are more shallow and ob-sessed with women having skinny or "perfect" bodies. Yet, when I am feeling positive and confident about my body, I tend to receive emails online from men who tell me they "love a woman with curves". I think it is about really owning and being cool with who we are. This includes the ability to look within and see our inner beauty and strengths, as well. I always speak and coach about women cultivating their inner strengths and talents, as well as their work and hobbies! We have to be in our power place enough to be able to say, "I don't care if I'm not the hottest, skinniest, youngest chick he is emailing online, because I KNOW that I...am smart; can hold a great con-versation; can pick an exquisite bottle of wine; know every player on the *Lakers*; am a great lover; and can make a delicious Lasagna!" One thing I do know for sure from reading a million dating books and dating plenty myself over the years is that men love CONFIDENT women! Once you impress a man with all your special qualities, I think the physical might take a back seat. Men also love women with SELF-RESPECT! I think this is the core of our Q&A today! If we respect ourselves, choose men online who respect us, say NO to requests that feel disrespectful (No texting or emailing naked photos!), remember our worth, and hold out for the respectful men we deserve, the emails from the shallow fools will just be fodder for us to laugh at!

DEAR BROOKE

FIANCE LIED ABOUT GOING TO A STRIP CLUB

MELISSA: I've been dating a wonderful man for two years who recently proposed to me. After a bachelor party in Vegas, my fiancé lied about going to a strip club. I told him from day one: NO STRIP CLUBS! After finding out, he gave me a speech about it being a bachelor party, Vegas, blah, blah, blah…and now every time he goes out with his friends, an argument erupts because I don't believe he's going where he says. Trust is important to me and I don't know how I'll marry him without it. I told him he has to call me a few times when he's out with friends. He thinks that's controlling. Am I being a controlling Drama Queen?

BROOKE: The answer is "YES!" and I am dropping your "Controlling Drama Queen" membership card into the mailbox! But, don't fret, because you'll be joining the club with millions of women, including *yours truly*. Trust is something I've been challenged, so I get it! Now, let's start with the fact that you opened your question with "I've been dating a wonderful man." I love that you wrote that and listen/look for things that show me the "bigger" picture. That leads me to believe that your fiancé hasn't shown you a pattern of lies prior to this strip club. The problem here is NOT that he went to the strip club, but that he broke an *agreement* that you made and *lied* to you about it! I am hearing you feel *betrayed* and *disrespected* and that's what this is about. I understand your feelings 100% (and, so do millions of readers whom have experienced this!). Did your fiancé CHOOSE to lie to you? Yes! But, I don't believe he did it to hurt you! He made his choice (a *wimpy* one!), hoping you wouldn't find out (Busted!). My advice is you start from scratch! Tell him how you feel (without making him *wrong*!), forgive him for lying to you and create a new agreement! How does it feel to give him freedom to hit a strip club ONLY for a Bachelor party? This doesn't mean he's cashing his check for 'singles' every Friday night! This compromise may satisfy you. I also want you to examine what this brings up for YOU! I've learned from past relationships, that situations like this challenge things that are going on deep within us. I remember when I dated a gorgeous film director and freaked-out every time he'd start a new film, because I assumed he'd want to sleep with his lead actress. I had to dig deep and figure out where MY insecurities were coming from. Was I comparing myself to these actresses? Was I not feeling good, pretty or talented enough? I realized it was my own *fear* of losing him. I share this, because I want you to dig deep and see if you're feeling fearful in some way? If so, I suggest you work on it with a coach! If your fiancé is the "wonderful" man you describe, then his hitting a strip club at a bachelor party shouldn't affect your relationship! You'll be ripping up your "Controlling Drama Queen" membership card before ya know it!

THE TEMPTED TALK

Q&A With Dating Expert Brooke Lewis

Newly Separated, Forty And Fabulous, Loves Shopping And Successful

Q: I'm newly separated and ready to get back out and date. Do you think women will understand that I am not looking for anything serious? - Joseph

A: Joseph, with today's high divorce rate, you are not alone! Like I always say, "There is someone or many "someones" for everyone!" I fully encourage you to get back into the dating world. I advise clients in your situation to simply be honest with yourself and others. When choosing online dating, choose a site (like Tempted!) that caters to users in similar places and situations. You do not want to join a dating site that is focused on members seeking a serious commitment or marriage. You will meet some wonderful women, but let them know you are looking for casual dates and fun at this time. No one can fault you for the truth. And, do not make yourself "wrong" for being where you are. Go enjoy a bunch of sexy women and before you know it, you might be ready for something more!

Q: Brooke, I just turned 40 and I still look pretty good, but I am so afraid men will not want to date me because of my age. Any advice? - Stephanie

A: Stephanie, haven't you heard that 40 is the new 20? ;) It is all about confidence, Girl! Now, embrace your beauty, both inside and out, and run to your closet, grab the sexiest dress and high heels you own, go get your hair and nails done and hit up the hottest 45-60 year old men to "TEMPT ME" with a night of fine dining! Take it from me, both personally and professionally, there is nothing better than a wonderful, loving and generous 50-year-old man who will adore you. And, just think, you will always be 10 years younger! ;)

Q: I am a 22-year-old model in Los Angeles. I am so sick of meeting guys on dating apps who think I am going to sleep with them just because they buy me a drink. I have another model friend who dates wealthy men who take her shopping and on trips and she does sleep with them. Do you think this is wrong? - Daphne

A: As a Life and Dating Coach, I have committed to not judging! And, believe me, I am no one to judge. Between my clients, friends and myself, there is nothing I have not heard or experienced. It seems today that most people online and digital dating are becoming intimate with one another quite quickly, especially with the younger generation, like yours. I believe in the old saying, "You are the only one who has to sleep on your pillow at night and wake up with yourself in the morning." I say you CHOOSE what works and feels good for you! I do not think there is anything "wrong" with dating a wealthy man who takes you shopping and the two of you being intimate, as long as you show each other respect. Empower yourself in whatever way makes you happy.

Q: I am a successful entrepreneur who travels for work three weeks out of each month. My commitment to work and travel has ruined several relationships. Do you really believe that is it possible for me to find an ongoing relationship or situation of some kind where the woman can travel with me? - Paul

A: Not only do I believe you can find a relationship with a travel companion, but I *KNOW* you can! I also understand how frustrating it can be to be married to your career, yet still have needs and love in your heart to give to another person. I do not think the traditional online dating route is for you and what you seek. At *Tempted.com*, the dating and relationship possibilities are endless! You want to "Tempt" and reach out to women who have freedom and flexibility! There are members who have just completed college and want to see the world before entering the workforce, members who do not have the financial means to travel, members who are not fulfilled by their work and would love to explore something/somewhere new and members who are divorced, were left with an abundant settlement, do not have to work and have all the time in the world (Naturally, you will want to take care of all travel and living expenses for your other half, while traveling.) So, get comfortable with that Travel icon and if you do not find the "One" to travel the rest of her days with you so quickly, I bet you will find quite a few passengers who would happily be tempted to travel with you for periods of time, until you do!

THE TEMPTED TALK

Q&A With Dating Expert Brooke Lewis

Respect, Younger Men, Multiple Men And Business Travel

Q: I'm a guy who respects women. I enjoy taking women out to nice dinners and events, but, sometimes, I get really frustrated when my friends tell me they are hooking up all the time and don't even take women out. I feel like I am doing the right thing, but I don't seem to be having the luck they are getting a woman back to bed. What am I doing wrong? - Devin

A: First, let me say that you are NOT doing anything WRONG! You sound like a true gentleman and that is whom most women seek. I really believe that it is all about timing and chemistry. I know a lot of women claim they do not sleep with men on the first few dates, but I can tell you from someone who hears it *all* from friends and clients, this is not always true. If the setting is right and a woman CHOOSES to sleep with you, she will. BUT, she has to WANT to! So, I would say we should examine your behavior from dinner on. Are you courting her enough? Are you being assertive enough? Are you being seductive enough? Are you letting her know what you want? I coach men and women NOT to have too many expectations on a date, but be honest about what you are seeking. And, remember, you can always come back and "Tempt" a woman with another date to travel for the weekend or come to your place for the fabulous bottle of wine (wink ;).

Q: I am in my 40s and love dating younger men. I have tried online dating sites and it seems most men are seeking younger women. Do you think I can have success looking for younger men online? - Sharon

A: Sharon, the good news for you is that there are so many people online dating now, you will find people with all different preferences. The other good news is that being a "Cougar" seems to be quite sexy and popular in our society today! I do want to tell you, honestly, that more times than not, men are online seeking younger women (especially in a big city…Hello, Los Angeles!), but this does not mean there are not plenty of options and possibilities for a beautiful, mature woman! My main piece of advice to you is that, besides adjusting your profile settings, you may want to be more of the aggressor when it comes to "tempting" or posting a "TEMPT" in The Playground. Let men know that you are seeking younger. You may even want to be the one to "Tempt" the younger guys with a drinks icon. I say put it out there! You have nothing to lose and you just may meet a man your age in the mix!

Q: I'm in my late 30s, was married for 15 years and want to be free and fun now. Is it wrong for me to date multiple men at once? - Amy

A: Amy, as a single, liberated, independent woman myself, I give you full permission to date as many men as you want to! I have been single forever and dated a lot! I have had so much fun, learned many lessons, learned a lot about men and, more importantly, a lot about myself. Sometimes, I think the most valuable lessons are learned through our mistakes. Learning to take care of yourself and your needs is very important. Just remember, be honest with yourself and others. Try the best you can to not hurt anyone along the way. I was always open and honest about letting men know that I was not dating them exclusively. Most of the time they appreciated the truth and other times, they chose not to see me anymore. But, I never misled anyone! With choices, there are consequences. Be smart and safe! Being sexual or intimate with more than one person at a time can be a tricky thing! Just follow your heart and you will know when you are ready to stop playing and start finding love again.

Q: Hey, Hollywood! I am coming to LA for business for two weeks and want to find a date and hit the town. Any suggestions? - Dominick

A: Yes! Take advantage of being a member of *Tempted.com* (LOL)! Since this is "Where Temptation and Dating Connect", you are in good digital hands. I can promise you that Hollywood has plenty to "Tempt" with and temptation that is hard to resist! If you have time to plan (or, have your assistant do it!), purchase tickets to a *Kings* game or a Broadway show at the *Pantages Theatre*. You cannot beat Beverly Hills or Malibu for the perfect meal. *Mastro's Ocean* or *Nobu* overlook the beach in Malibu and set the tone for a very romantic night. You can't beat *The Palm* or *Wolfgang Steakhouse* in Beverly Hills, then drinks at *The Peninsula Hotel*. And, if you want more of a Hollywood scene, hit *BOA* Sunset, then drinks above at the famous *SOHO House*. I don't think there is a lady in town who will not be up for this type of temptation. In fact, if you get stuck, I know a Dating Expert at *Tempted.com* who loves to fine dine (wink wink ;). JK!

THE TEMPTED TALK

Q&A With Dating Expert Brooke Lewis

DIVORCED DAD, SUGAR DADDY, SPORTING EVENTS AND TEMPT ME

Q: I am a divorced Dad with three kids under 10. I do not have a ton of time to date or start a serious relationship. Would I find something casual on Tempted? - Robert

A: As a single woman who has enjoyed dating divorced Dads, I can promise you that *Tempted.com* is the site for you! This site is the place to be direct and honest about your dating needs, without apologies. You can find something as serious or casual, as you seek. If you feel all you have to give at this time is a Saturday night for dinner, when you do not have your kids, you can "Tempt" a woman with just that. If you are seeking something casual, but ongoing, you can "Tempt" and connect with a woman with similar interests or whom is in a similar situation. We are in the space we are in, until we are no longer in it. You can definitely find many situations and experiences here that will work for where you are right now.

Q: A few of my friends are on the "Sugar Daddy" style dating sites. I thought about joining, but it just feels weird to me to think of myself as a "Sugar Baby". I found your site and I am wondering how it is different? - Lacey

A: Lacey, I really love your question and have had several other women inquire about the differences between "Sugar" sites and *Tempted.com*. I believe that with all dating and dating sites, there is an agreement in some way, shape or form. Someone contacts another and agreements are created from a date to a relationship to a simple hookup! I also know that specific sites are designed for different types of dating agreements. I do not judge and I do not think there is anything wrong with "Sugar-style" dating, but I do not think it is for everyone! If you choose a "Sugar-style" dating site, choose it powerfully and make sure you feel good about it. At *Tempted.com*, we have designed a way to date where anything is possible. One day, you can "ACCEPT" a "TEMPT" from that millionaire who is visiting from Texas and wants to take you to a black tie event, while buying you the dress, shoes and purse to go with it and the next day, you can you can "ACCEPT" a date for coffee with the cute musician whose profile you checked out three times. *Tempted.com* really does empower women to set their own rules and if being a "Sugar Baby" gives you a cavity, you can hit the "TEMPT ME" button for what makes you feel good!

Q: It seems like a lot of successful men have season tickets to sporting events. I am not a sports fan, but sometimes pretend to be, so men will invite me to a game. Do you think this is a bad thing? - Kelly

A: Kelly, this is an interesting question and I think a lot of people "pretend" a lot of things when they are dating and online dating. I actually think it is a great thing when someone steps out of his/her comfort zone to try something new. As a woman who loves sports, I also know how much fun a live game can be! I get concerned when people begin dating and they are not true to THEMSELVES! When a person pretends to be someone or something he/she is not, it creates a false perception and he/she enters the situation or experience with a lie. At times, one lie can spin into several lies, then you get into trouble. I would love to see you try a different approach to this. I suggest you let the next guy who asks you (or "Tempts" you with!) to a sporting event know that you are NOT the biggest sports fan, BUT that you would like to attend to keep him company and enjoy a fun time doing something he loves! I guarantee that tiny bit of honesty will show a guy how cool you really are and help you win his heart!

Q: Expert, I need your HELP! I keep putting myself out there and inviting men to "TEMPT ME". I am not having a great response or much luck. What do I do? - Connie

A: Connie, I am here to tell you that you are not alone! There are women who feel this way and, believe it or not, many men who feel this way. I have heard this concern over many years from many clients on different dating sites. I think the most important things to do when online dating is to be PERSISTENT, CONFIDENT and...REALISTIC!

Remember, there are many "someones" for everyone when online dating. With so many online daters, users' choices are endless. However, I do believe the words I mentioned above are essential. Do not give up and be patient enough to allow the "right" dates to come. I say put it out there, but know when to sit back for a moment and not be too aggressive. Be realistic in your choices and with whom you might be most compatible. Believe in yourself and TRUST that your dates will come. I have always found that when I stop trying and working so hard, things and love magically appear.

THE TEMPTED TALK

Q&A With Dating Expert Brooke Lewis

Wild Side, Wealthy Men, Online Dating and A Career Woman

Q: I have been dating a guy I met online and I am really into him. My concern is he seems to have a wild side. He asked me to make out with another girl for him at a club the other night and has suggested swapping with another couple. I'm not sure how I feel about this. Any advice? - "Confused"

A: Okay, "Confused"! First, allow me to give you permission to be confused. You have every right to feel what you feel, so allow yourself to be with it. As a Coach, I try not to pass judgment and, remember, at *Tempted.com*, we do not pass judgment, either, and support each member's wants and needs. That said, I support you in doing whatever it is (or, is not!) that makes you feel good about yourself. If you are curious about something and think it might bring you joy, test the waters. If you think something will cause you to feel shame or embarrassment, make a different choice. Whatever you do, just make sure you are doing it for yourself and the right reasons. Do not do something that will make you feel lousy to gain or keep the love of another person. Stay true to yourself. And, there are plenty of wild and sexy things couples can do that do not involve others or something that makes you feel "confused".

Q: I have been dating a woman I am crazy about for a few months. She is beautiful and really cool. My issue is that she has a track record of dating extremely wealthy men. I am financially comfortable, but by no means "rich". I find myself spending more money than I should and am afraid I will not be able to keep her in the lifestyle she is accustomed to. What do I do? - Dan

A: I have to tell you, I appreciate your position and think I can be of great help here. Dan, I, too, have dated a lot of wealthy men in my dating career and I swear to you, I would choose a financially "comfortable" guy who loves, respects and adores me over an extremely wealthy guy who does not, any day! Just because your girl has dated very rich men, does not mean they all treated her well or were there for her emotionally. I have dated some wealthy men who worked so many hours, I hardly got to see them, while others were so arrogant and self-absorbed, they never asked a single question about my life or career. I do not want to generalize here, but make a point that money does not always create happiness. Now, that also does not mean that I would not prefer to date someone who is financially sound, but you shared that you are and I am pretty sure, by now, your girl knows your status. Do not be insecure and do the best you can with what you have! And, if your girl turns out to show "gold digger" colors down the road, then re-evaluate this relationship and shoot me another advice question. My advice will be a bit different!

Q: I'm new to online dating and *Tempted.com*. As the Expert, can you please tell me how to ease into this? - George

A: George, first allow me to welcome you to *Tempted.com*! Also, know that you are welcome to reach out to me any time for Expert advice at our site. You have joined a dating site that was created to bring you fun and excitement, so let's ease you in! I say to dive in, but swim slowly. Since you are new to online dating, you will want to learn the basics, then try to learn the online dating culture and different behaviors and personalities you will be dealing with. I suggest for your first "Tempt" and date, try the coffee icon. Keep it simple and get a feel for the process of speaking to, then meeting, a person you have never seen before. Make sure you actually talk (not text!) with your date ahead of time and make a quick plan to spend an hour or so getting to know each other over a latte. You have nothing to lose except time and you may just make a new friend. On a super positive note, you may be so insanely attracted to one another, you will grab your phone the minute you get back into your car and "Tempt" that person with a drinks, dinner and show extravaganza the following night. Temptation and dating tend to connect here at Tempted!

Q: As a total career woman, would *Tempted.com* be an

appropriate dating place for me? - Kendall

A: Kendall, you are preaching to the choir! I totally get your position and the frustration around dating as a career focused woman. And, YES! *Tempted.com* is a fabulous place for you! We can examine the reasons from two different perspectives. First, I coach a lot of successful women who prefer to date successful men. If you have pampered yourself with the finer things in life (because you have worked hard for them!), there is no reason you should not expose yourself to successful men who want to pamper you too! The second perspective is that more and more successful women are focusing on their careers and earning financial rewards, so they do not need a man to support them. These women prefer to be in control and run the show and have no problem treating a man to show or hockey tickets. If you want to "Tempt" a guy for that game date, go for it! I suggest posting your "TEMPT" in The Playground, as I am willing to bet you'll have more men falling at your sneakers than you ever imagined!

THE TEMPTED TALK
Q&A With Dating Expert Brooke Lewis

ROMANCE, STUDENT ON A BUDGET, SEX AND A CAR

Q: I am a single guy who is back in the dating game. I am trying to be more romantic this time. Any suggestions? - Marc

A: Well, Marc, you have come to the right place and person! I am a forever "hopeful romantic" and having dated a lot, I've experienced some wonderful romantic gestures from men. I want to start by saying that romance does not have to be about money. Some of my most romantic dates were quite simple. I am a sucker for cards and my favorite *Godiva Chocolates*. I believe romance begins with thought! I dated one guy who knew I was into spiritual things and actually bought me a STAR in the sky! I've also dated very successful men who planned a weekend away to an exotic resort, and another who surprised me with a new TV. The romance here was NOT about the expense of the new TV, but the THOUGHT behind the fact that I had expressed that my old TV was not working well and he listened, remembered and created a solution! Another solution is for you to go to *Tempted.com* and take many romantic opportunities the site offers, from a night of fine-dining to travel…Fiji, here we come!

Q: As a single graduate student in my 20s, I am on a budget and seeking to date men who want to buy me some things I cannot afford. I am not sure how to approach this. Can you help me? - Nikki

A: Nikki, as a Life Coach, I am trained to hear things underneath what is actually said. I am hearing that you are feeling a bit uncomfortable about asking for what you want and need. This is totally understandable and a lot of women feel this way. One of the things I am passionate about representing with *Tempted.com*, is that we have created a site for HONEST dating! Rather than wasting time, "beating around the bush," you have a platform to invite what you want. Women are empowered, and welcome, to use the "TEMPT" button at any time to invite a man to ask them out for a dinner or SHOPPING date! Do not worry about what people think of you and go after what you want! You may end up with a new *Dior* bag on one arm and a wonderful guy on the other!

Q: I went on a Tempted date last night and really liked her. I am taking her out again Saturday night. I am really sexually attracted to her and want to spend the night with her. Will she be offended if I plan an overnight date? - Phil

A: Phil, I have a feeling you are not the only guy wanting an answer to this question (LOL)! Listen, we are all adults here and we make our own choices. That said, not everyone makes (or, is ready to make) the same choice at the same time. If you are asking me if there is anything "wrong" with being sexual on the second date, I will tell you, I have no problem with it. BUT, I am not your date! The answer to this one lies completely in communication. Be honest and communicate with your date! Most importantly, make her feel comfortable with your plan. I have dated men who I knew I was interested in being sexual with early on and others who I chose to wait quite some time. I also do not think an overnight date MUST involve sex! I have taken weekend trips with men I dated, had plenty of romance and did not become sexual. I have also gone away with men and requested a second hotel room. Again, this is all about communication with your date. Discuss the overnight plan with her and ask how she feels. Do not force anything and allow things to move at their own natural pace. Hey, Phil! She may surprise you and be even friskier than you Saturday night (LOL)! Have fun!

Q: Brooke, I need your Expert HELP! I have been dating a very wealthy guy for three months. He just offered to buy me a car! I want to accept this so badly, but I am so afraid I will owe him, if I do. - Carly

A: Carly, I am glad you asked this question, because I think a lot of women struggle with the feeling of "owing" someone something, if a person does something nice for them! I have definitely struggled with this over the years and really had to work hard on breaking this emotional pattern. When someone offers us a generous gift, we want to accept it with appreciation and gratitude. We also want to understand that the other person CHOSE to give us that generous gift. It is our choice whether to ACCEPT it or not. My best advice is to learn whether a man is giving you something from his heart or if he is giving you something through control or manipulation. Rather than thinking about it, I would like you to "feel" if it is good for you or not. Your gut will usually guide you to the right answer. And, if you accept the car, just make sure he puts it in your name (LOL)!

THE TEMPTED TALK

Q&A With Dating Expert Brooke Lewis

Long-Distance, Social Media, D*ck Pics And The Valley

Q: I'm a newly divorced guy who wants to date outside of the area where my wife and I lived for 20 years. Do you think this will work? - Kevin

A: I think long-distance dating can absolutely work IF both parties are honest about who they are and what they want. I think that people who are looking for long-term relationships or marriage have issues to address and communicate, beyond what you will be dealing with any time soon. So, as for you, I think long-distance dating will be a great choice! I think after a long marriage or commitment, you owe it to yourself to find *you* again and have some fun! You are not the same person you were 20 years ago and, I promise you, dating is definitely not the same as it was back then (LOL)! I can tell you from my own experiences, that long-distance dating can be a blast and serve the purpose you are seeking. You don't want any major commitments right now, nor heavy expectations on you or your time, so having a fling or a few month wonderful rendezvous is perfect. Of course, you have come to the right place at *Tempted.com*. I suggest you plan a fun-filled weekend away for yourself, add a plus one to all your reservations and "Tempt" some sexy lady you connect with to join your weekend of adventure!

Q: I have been dating a guy exclusively and something is driving me crazy! We are both late 20s and he says he wants something more than just casual, but he is on social media all day long. I see his posts on *Facebook* and *Instagram* and it makes me not trust him. He is constantly in photos and flirting with other women. He says it is harmless and they are friends, but it upsets me and I don't know what to do? - April

A: April, I totally understand and sympathize with you and your situation. I have been there and this is not fun. I speak a lot about how I feel social media is a blessing and a curse. Honestly, I would not want to be in my 20s again and having to deal with this. That said, you are, so let's find the best way to address it. I would like to know if he EVER posts photos of the two of you together? What is his relationship *status* on *Facebook*? Are his photos with other women fun and playful or are they crossing the boundaries of two people in an exclusive relationship? Regardless of the answers, only you feel what you feel. Honor those feelings. Trust your instincts. If you feel there is a reason to be concerned, communicate with your man and see if he makes any changes. If not, start browsing *Tempted.com* again. Here at Tempted, we know that communication is key.

Q: As a woman who is actively online dating, I am getting disgusted with the number of men who are texting me "d*ck pics". Some do it before ever meeting me! Brooke, how do I respond to this? - Katie

A: I am so glad you asked this question, because so many women want to know the answer. I have clients and girlfriends who address this with me every day. I have experienced this more times than I would like to remember and I took the extreme approach and deleted and blocked every guy who texted me "d*ck pics". For me, that is a sure sign of disrespect! That said, this approach serves me, but I want to be fair and objective to others. I have always preached that the mere fact that men believe this behavior is okay, means that somewhere in the past, a woman allowed it and made it acceptable. I will also share that I know women who have admitted they are turned on by this! Now, you want to figure out a response that works for you. I coach each person to make her own rules. Another approach is to let the guy know immediately that this behavior makes you uncomfortable and that the guy you want to date would not send naked pics. Give the guy a chance to explain. He might surprise you and respect your wishes from that point on. One thing I enjoy about *Tempted.*

com is that you can be yourself and be honest about searching for what/whom you want. If you want something casual or sexy, it is easy to find. If you want something to move slowly, do a coffee "TEMPT". It makes is simple to set boundaries that are right for you!

Q: I will be on business in LA and staying in Encino. Are there any good date spots or do I need to drive to Beverly Hills for dinner? I have heard about your rush hour traffic. - Ted

A: Ted, you came to the right Expert. I have been wined and dined for both business and pleasure, so I am happy to guide you. First of all, the place we call "The Valley" has grown and expanded great-ly. I recommend checking out all the delicious restaurants nearby. You can "Tempt" a darling with fine dining and take her to *Mastro's* Woodland Hills. For more casual, but tasty fare, you can *Uber* it over to Studio City and bar and restaurant jump from *Firefly to Granville to Ceremony.* I say you "Tempt" a date to drinks, then see where the night takes you. Of course, taking her from drinks to dinner in a limo never hurts either, and you will not even be thinking about our dread-ful traffic!

ABOUT THE AUTHOR

I feel blessed to be one of those people who discovered her life purpose very early on. I was the product of divorced parents by the age of two and dealt with chronic health challenges and body image issues, since childhood. I was a shy and insecure kid who was afraid to be "me" or have a "voice". I never felt "good enough". I had no idea how "powerful" I was or how "powerful" I would one day become as an adult. I only wish I had a mentor or coach to help me discover it back then. I was extremely empathic, intuitive and sensitive to people's feelings and experiences. I learned to channel those feelings through creativity and performing. I was acting, singing and dancing by the age of eight.

By high school, I developed a strong sense of self and graduated in the top of my class. By college, I was President of my sorority, winning National awards and scholarships and graduated Magna Cum Laude. I planned to go to Law School, but followed my true calling and headed to New York to be an actress. Instead of following logic, I followed my life purpose. I made my living acting in New York for a few years and headed out to Hollywood. I achieved some wonderful success as an actress and went on to become an independent producer and created *Philly Chick Pictures*. I became an award-winning actress and producer and even found fame in the horror genre. In that genre, I also found the most amazing creation of my career...*Ms. Vampy*.

I had always felt that I was being of service to others through my acting, but I felt like I needed to make a difference on a deeper level. I have been through so much in my life and I still feel like a teenager at heart, so I created a talk show for teens with *Ms. Vampy* as a role model to mentor them through issues they face today. The show was such an inspiration that I found my other true calling and went back to school to further pursue my understanding and certification as a Life Coach. I later launched my coaching company *Be You And Be Fearless Life Coach*.

While staying true and committed to my passions and dreams, I have always remained a "love bug". I chose my career over marriage, but still remain a "hopeful romantic". As a single woman in La La Land, I have actually had the time of my life dating and online dating, and have stories to fill a volume of books! As my Life Coaching business grew, I learned how many people are challenged with dating, online dating, getting back out "there" after a break-up or a divorce and how much digital dating has changed the natural course of finding love and a partner. My clients would come in to break through a career fear and half the coaching session would turn into a conversation about the date they had the night before. I am so excited and inspired by the subject of dating and online dating (and, surely skilled on the subject!), that I expanded my coaching career and became a Dating Coach and Expert. We know that dating requires us to be "dauntless", so, as a coach, I am here to help you **BE YOU...AND, BE FEARLESS!**

CREDENTIALS:

Life Coach Certification- The Life Purpose Institute Program (LPI) founded in 1984, was one of the first life coach training schools to pioneer the life coaching field and offer Life Coach Certification. Its coaching tools and methods have successfully been utilized with over one million people worldwide. The Life Purpose Institute provides an extensive Life Coach Certification program to train you to become a competent and successful Life Coach.

Board Certified Coach, BCC- The Center for Credentialing & Education (CCE) created the Board Certified Coach (BCC) credential as a means to independently verify that applicants have met professional coaching competency standards established by CCE and subject matter experts. These standards reflect the common knowledge, skills and abilities of a professional coach.

The BCC is a mark of quality. It demonstrates to the public that a professional coach has:

-Met educational and training requirements

-Passed a psychometrically sound coach-specific examination

-Obtained experience in the field of coaching

-Professional peer references

-Accountability to an enforceable ethics code

-Commitment to continuing education

Bachelor's Degree- Rhetoric and Communications from Temple University

-Rhetoric- the art and study of the use of language with persuasive effect.

-Speech Communications- public speaking; the vocalized form of human communication.

-Interpersonal Communication- the process that we use to communicate our ideas, thoughts and feelings to another person.

BROOKE LEWIS BIO

A native of Philadelphia, the vivacious and versatile Brooke Lewis has made an impact as an actress, producer and TV personality. Brooke relocated to New York, where she began her professional career. Her first major taste of the limelight came from *Tony n' Tina's Wedding* - the Off-Broadway hit comedy- in which she played the "prima donna" bridesmaid Donna Marsala. Brooke would also find success on-screen, appearing in *The Rules (For Men)*, *A Packing Suburbia* and *Pride & Loyalty*.

She headed west - to Hollywood. There, she would create Philly Chick Pictures, an endeavor designed to increase opportunities in front of the camera, as well as behind it. Since making the move, Brooke has had roles in, or on, several projects, including, *Quintuplets*, *Mafiosa*, *Break*, *Gerald*, *Dahmer Vs. Gacy*, *Alien Dawn*, *The Mourning*, *Starship: Rising*, *Starship: Apocalypse* and *Lazarus Apocalypse*. Some of this firecracker's impressive producing credits include: *Broken Angel* (co-producer), *Kinky Killers* (actress/co-executive producer), *iMurders* (actress/executive producer), *The Drum Beats Twice* (actress/executive producer), *The Sinatra Club* (actress/producer), *Slime City Massacre* (actress/co-producer) and *Sprinkles* (actress/executive producer/producer).

In 2009, Brooke launched the *Ms. Vampy* TV/talk show/web series, which she created, starred in and produced. In 2011, Brooke followed with the teen smash hit TV/talk show/web series *Ms. Vampy's Tween Tawk, Teen Tawk & In Between Tawk*, which won the HONOLULU FILM AWARDS 2012 SILVER LEI AWARD and the coveted 18TH ANNUAL COMMUNICATOR AWARDS (2012) AWARD OF DISTINCTION for Social Responsibility and in 2014, *Ms. Vampy's Love Bites* won the HONOLULU FILM AWARDS BEST TV PILOT AWARD. She was honored by Screamqueen.com as SCREAM QUEEN OF THE MONTH November 2008. SCARS MAGAZINE honored her with the centerfold and interview in March 2009 and she graced the

October 2009 Cover of SCARS MAGAZINE with *iMURDERS* Co-star Tony Todd. "VOGUE for Horror Fans" GOREZONE MAGAZINE chose her as their celebrity GOREMATE August 2010. Spreading out to SciFi, she is SIRIUS Satellite Radio's SLICE OF SCIFI's SLICE QUEEN. Brooke was honored by the B MOVIE GOLDEN COB AWARDS 2010 for BEST SCREAM QUEEN of 2009. Brooke won the PollyGrind Film Festival 2011 BEST ACTRESS IN A SHORT FILM AWARD and the Action On Film International Film Festival 2011 honored her with the prestigious WRITE BROTHERS EXCELLENCE IN FILM AND VIDEO AWARD. In 2012, Brooke gratefully graced the October 2014 Cover of TALENT MONTHLY MAGAZINE.

Inspired by her teen talk show, she went back to school in 2011 and Brooke became an award-winning Board Certified Life Coach and Dating and Online Dating Coach and Expert. She has done writing, speaking and TV segments in media such as *San Diego Living CW6, CBS 8 Las Vegas Now, John Kerwin Live, AfterBuzz TV, Pop Trigger TV, Huffington Post, She Knows, Your Tango, Dirty And Thirty, Girls Life, Woman's Day, Female First* and *Meet Mindful*. Brooke is also known as the sassy Co-host on the dating talk show *Breaking Dating*. Brooke earned the title *Tempted Dating Expert & Spokesperson* in January 2016, after helping to "revamp" the online dating site. She has empowered women and men around the world, giving them knowledge they can use in their everyday lives and giving them the confidence they need to go after dating, love and their dreams. Her motto is...BE FEARLESS!

As if she is not busy enough, Brooke strongly believes in charity work that empowers women and young adults. She was chosen HOT HUNKS OF HORROR HOTTIE 2009. The amazing "hunky horror" calendar benefits the Lynn Sage Foundation for Breast Cancer Research. She is also on DREAD CENTRAL's BOWLING FOR BOOBIES HORROR STARLETS Team to raise money and awareness for Busted Foundation and Breast Cancer. She speaks out against Bullying and was a Celebrity Judge at the 2014 NO BULL TEEN VIDEO AWARDS. Brooke is a proud member of Women In Film and Film Independent. And, during football season (when she finally decides to take a break from working!), you will always find her at a sports bar cheering for the Philadelphia EAGLES!

ACKNOWLEDGEMENTS

As an Actress, Scream Queen, Producer, Writer, Speaker, Board Certified Life Coach, Dating Coach and Expert, TV Personality, Talk Show Host, *Ms. Vampy*, Empowered Single Woman and Hot Mess, I have had so many careers and life experiences, I feel like I really have lived "Vampire" years! If there is one thing I have learned from my experiences, failures, mistakes and successes, it is that none of it would be possible without the love and support of the people in our lives! Life is challenging and our friends and family can drive us nuts (I know I have driven mine nutty!), but I could not have gotten this far without them! I have been truly blessed with the most wonderful, loving (and, sometimes nutty!) family, friends, career reps, business associates, clients and fans in the *Universe*! Please know how grateful I am for YOU and, although I am married to my work and career goals most of the time, I always send you love and light from afar!

As you can imagine, there are too many amazing and important people in my *Universe* to mention, but I need to shout out to a few whom have guided me through this HOT MESS journey:

My Family: Who has given me "undying" love and support, even if it has taken me "Vampire" years to get here! And, who has loved me through ALL my HOT MESSES!

My Friends: From Philly to Jersey to New York to Los Angeles, who have remained a constant source of grounding, encouragement and loyalty and never let me forget where I came from!

My Spiritual Healers: Marilyn Alauria, Lori Bertazzon, Karen

Abrams and Gila Varis who have shared their healing gifts with me to keep me "healthy" on my path to success!

My Reps: Bohemia Group, Katz Public Relations, Media Artists Group, Meyer & Downs, and Coolwaters Productions. For believing in me and my talents through the ebbs and flows of this Hollywood crazy train!

My Photographer and Hair & Make-up Artists: Birdie Thompson and Glamourax, whose skills transformed me for the photos in this book!

My Genie: Mark, who has made me believe again and made all my wishes come true!

Thank you to all of the above, fans and readers for allowing me to *BE FEARLESS* and embrace my *HOT MESS*!

www.ingramcontent.com/pod-product-compliance
Lightning Source LLC
Chambersburg PA
CBHW070019300526

45794CB00001B/369